T0195860

The *Little* *Blue Room*

AWAKENING THE SOUL TO LOVE, JOY, FREEDOM, AND POWER

PAULINE RAPHAELA

BALBOA.PRESS

A DIVISION OF HAY HOUSE

Balboa Press books may be ordered through booksellers or by contacting:

Balboa Press
A Division of Hay House
1663 Liberty Drive
Bloomington, IN 47403
www.balboapress.com
844-682-1282

Print information available on the last page.

ISBN: 979-8-7652-2994-1 (sc)
ISBN: 979-8-7652-2996-5 (hc)
ISBN: 979-8-7652-2995-8 (e)

Library of Congress Control Number: 2022911268

Balboa Press rev. date: 09/20/2022

Lou,
For your infinite love, support, and belief in me.

Eternally Grateful

To My Beloved.

You cannot fill me up with joy
For I Am all the joy I need.

You cannot fill me up with love
For I Am all the love I need.

You cannot complete me
For I Am already completed.

You have given me the extraordinary experience of
true growth and awakening.

For it is you who taught me how to love myself.
It is you who taught me how to fill myself with joy.
It is you who taught me how to complete myself.

You were the mirror to awaken my Soul.

For this experience I am eternally grateful.

Pauline Raphaela

CONTENTS

Preface

The idea to write about the journey of awakening came directly from Spirit. I never before thought about writing a book, so the complete inspiration is from my spirit guides, who seem to think the information herein will help others on their own journeys to find the same things I longed for: true love, joy, power, and freedom.

The first time I received an inspiration to write was several weeks before I actually sat down and started typing. During this time, I felt a presence standing behind me, pushing on my left shoulder. Every time I felt that push, the word "Write" would pounce into my mind. At first, I ignored it as I truly thought it was nothing. What would I write about?

One day while relaxing, enjoying a cup of tea in my living room, the inspiration came on so strong it could not be ignored. I was literally pushed off the living room couch and whisked downstairs, almost floating into my computer room. With no idea or expectation about what would happen next, I sat down the morning of May 10, 2003, and started to type. My fingers moved so fast, my mind went blank, as if to get out of the way of the creative process.

The information flowed from my memory into my fingers and formed the beginning of what seemed to be a book. Three and a half hours elapsed before I realized what took place, but it felt like only twenty minutes. I stopped typing and thought about what had just occurred. The whole experience was slightly confusing. Looking at the newly typed material, it appeared to be my journey of awakening. Feelings of uncertainty were followed by questions such as, "Who me? Write a book?" The guidance was strong and certain. What was uncertain was the belief in myself.

At that moment a wave of cold energy swept over me. My body temperature dropped. I was shivering, and my bones felt cold as ice. This was not the first time the warmth of my human body vanished, and instantly I knew it was Spirit working through me, guiding the way.

Smiling with gratitude, I sank into the chair and relaxed. Feelings of inspiration and love filled my heart. "Okay ... okay. I will follow along," I blurted out to whoever was listening. Then I ran upstairs to take a steaming hot shower!

The purpose of this book is to inspire you to begin your own healing process, do the necessary Soul work, and awaken to the reason you are alive. All life experiences are excellent mirrors through which healing and evolution can occur. The human condition presents challenges that bring heartache as well as joy. But at the core, we all want the same things—love, joy, freedom, and power. These qualities can only be authentically created and shared with others when the Soul is awakened. This book presents such a mirror.

I pray this writing successfully assists humanity on its journey of awakening the Soul. The time is now, to consciously step up on the ladder of evolution, step into our divine hearts, and unify as people who help people, whose vision is to collectively create Heaven on Earth.

The information in these chapters is from a Soul perspective and will challenge the current way of thinking and being. I invite you to adopt the concepts presented herein and give yourself the gift of awakening. This book is for the meek, as they are the ones who will inherit the Earth.

Blessings in love,
Pauline Raphaela

INTRODUCTION

We dream of a peaceful world, one in which every living thing thrives. We dream of freedom and love and how we might create abundance for all life on our planet. Is our dream possible?

Yes! Evolution is occurring, and the call to awaken to our true natures is stronger than ever. Mysteries for the reason of our existence can now be explored through spirituality, with an understanding of who we are as Souls and what our Souls need to do while merged with human DNA.

Our lives consist of myriad experiences, some of which are pleasant, and others not. At one point or another we're all going to experience a situation that becomes the catalyst to jolt us out of our normal, limited views of life and who we are, into a higher understanding of the Soul self and why we are here. It could be the death of a loved one, a divorce, disease, or a tragic event that occurs in a local community or the world. We wonder why these events happen. We wonder what we could have done to prevent them. Logical solutions help in limited ways but rarely provide the long-term results we yearn for in our hearts.

These circumstances are meant to wake us up. They are meant to get us to start paying attention to something greater, bigger, and more profound than our understanding of who we think we are. There is a living being within all of us longing to be known, longing to be awakened, longing to change the world. That being is created from divine essence and is your Soul. Your glorious, magnificent, loving Soul.

What would it take to befriend this divine part of you?

Human life is challenging. Most of us carry wounds from early childhood, and those wounds are compounded in adulthood. We carry hereditary patterns in the form of behaviors, addictions, and disease. We've not been taught about our magnificent Souls or how to co-create with a loving and powerful Universe. We've followed the earthly path, and it has not brought us what we yearn for. As we grew up, we became more disconnected from God. We forgot about how the laws of energy, perfect health, and abundance really work. This has caused our lives to result in struggle, hardship, disease, war, and poverty. When we are disconnected from our God, we create chaos, separation, and lack.

But there is a way to change all this. There is a way to heal those wounds and become the loving, powerful being you were created to be. It's time to reconnect.

What must we do? We must heal our shadow sides, the wounds, the hurts, the anger, and hatred. We must embrace this part of us for it longs to be loved and healed by us. Being in the world makes us all part of mass consciousness. Every shadow aspect we see in the world is part of us in some way.

Why do we fear such deep healing?

We have not been taught about the true power of our Souls' divine love. The ego fears this love and prefers to stay in the same old patterns—such as insecurity, intolerance, and separation—simply because it's easier, and familiar. We've been taught to remain small and insignificant. Staying in shadow releases the ego from taking full responsibility for itself. It's challenging to rise above the lower patterns of the ego because it takes courage and determination to explore the true power of love, joy, and freedom.

Delving into the Soul's divine nature is an unknown experience, and the ego fears what it doesn't know or what it cannot control. Healing the shadow self automatically opens the door for the Soul to awaken. We fear our divine nature more than we fear staying in what is perceived to be comfortable.

When we awaken the love of our divine Soul, true power is awakened, but we have yet to understand just how transformational this will be. Our minds and bodies are just beginning to learn how to hold the highest vibration of divine love.

The present moment is an important time in human evolution to take part in the healing of our shadow self and awakening to the Soul self. Awakening your Soul is the only way in which peace, love, and unity will prevail.

Transformation from our shadows into Soul consciousness is within our reach. All Souls are needed to manifest such a reality. No Soul is insignificant, no Soul unneeded. Every Soul matters, especially yours. What impact will your personal awakening have on a family level, a community level, and a global level? The impact will be enormous. *Your* awakening is that essential!

The great spirits of love and peace hear our call. These energies slowly descend upon us. We must reach up and touch it, feel it, and embody it for this is how these energies will work through us. We live in the dimension of energy where "doing" and "creating" are the cornerstones of change, and change must first come from within. Each of us must become love, peace, and abundance for the world to reflect such qualities.

We are here on Earth now for one reason, to contribute to the evolution of life on Earth through a collective awakening. As I journeyed deep within myself, following the longings for material success, emotional stability, and loving relationships, I discovered that all I truly longed for was love, and all that I am—is love itself. Awakening to the love and joy of my Soul has transformed my life. I love more deeply, give more generously, and have more compassion for people. The victim no longer dwells inside me. Nor do feelings of powerlessness or insecurity rule my life. Once true power awakens, freedom abounds, and the need to control or blame someone or something does not exist. The strength of my higher self remains calm in a chaotic world. My love of humanity, animals, and every living creature is so strong that I must serve the greater good of evolution, for what other purpose is there?

In this time of great unrest and turmoil, awakening your Soul not only will change how you live, it is an essential part of bringing people together so that we all will live in abundance and peace. The conscious choice to awaken your Soul is the greatest gift you give yourself and the world as you contribute to life's evolution and transformation. As you read this book, be prepared to embody a greater sense of inner love, joy, freedom, and power along with a desire to serve! Let's begin the journey of awakening.

Chapter 1

The Ultimate Opportunity

Why do we need to experience circumstances that jolt us or break our hearts? Wouldn't it be better if we could avoid such pain? The answer is no. Crisis offers us the ultimate opportunity for personal growth as it is meant to set our feet on a path of self-discovery. Oftentimes crisis pushes us to seek therapy or counseling to heal strong emotions such as grief or anger. "Why did this happen to me?" is the question we seek answers to.

Beyond emotional healing is a message. Understanding why something happened the way it did and accepting that sometimes these situations must occur as catalysts to begin a new cycle of life is empowering. A new cycle offers the ultimate opportunity to know more about who you are at the Soul level and why you exist. There is a message behind every crisis waiting to be explored by everyone affected by it, whether it is personal or global.

Without the mirror of crisis, there may well be no impetus to seek healing or to reconnect with God or each other. To remain the victim or to refuse to see the larger picture of these circumstances will only continue the cycle of personal and global crises. That's why we must understand how these cycles play out in a deeper way.

For me, several personal crises were the catalyst for the greatest journey of my life. All I ever longed for was to awaken the love, joy, freedom, and power of my Soul, but I didn't know that until the death of my father caused me to spiral downward into darkness and explore the unknown. I was challenged to look at life, myself, and who I really longed to be. Not until that devastating crisis did I start paying attention to what creates all living things—God. Not until the passing of a man I loved deeply and relied on did I start asking the deep questions, such as "Who am I?" and "Why am I here?" The mirror of life was staring me in the face, suggesting that being courageous enough to look into it would provide healing, personal power, and answers to questions pertaining to the mystery of life.

The Crisis

The journey started on July 8, 1988, a humid night in the thick of a sweltering New York City summer. When my husband and I arrived home to our cozy one-bedroom apartment on the fifth floor of a pre-World War II building, I had no idea what was about to unfold. I knew only that our building, with its old-world architecture, solid brick structure with plaster walls, elegant archways, and hardwood floors, gave me a sense of safety and protection from the outside world. But that night, as I put the key in the door, the phone was ringing. It was nine-thirty at night, too late for a friendly call, and my adrenaline surged. My gut twisted as I dashed for the phone.

"Pauline, I've been trying to call you all evening." It was my stepmother, Brigitte.

My father had been sick for two years. He and Brigitte had been living in a high-rise apartment building in Florida, with breathtaking views overlooking the Intracoastal Waterway. Every time I visited I was struck by the beauty of the panoramic vista of an aqua ocean blessed with palm trees swaying in the wind. Sadly, my father did not have the chance to enjoy the beauty. Most of his time was spent in a stark-white hospital room. My visits consisted of watching him float in and out of consciousness, attached to tubes and machines that kept him alive.

When he was awake, his eyes were glued to the television as he focused on the stock market fluctuations. "Do you know how much money I could be making right now if I weren't in here?" he asked repeatedly. What could I say to comfort him? I shook my head as I watched him watch TV and pretended to understand the complex nature of trading and stock markets. His bed was near a window. My mind would drift off as I looked out at the blue Florida sky. I sat by his side, feeding him watermelon and oranges, which were his favorite sources of liquid nutrition.

"When I get out of here, I'm going to have an orgy with fruit!" he exclaimed. My heart broke watching this savvy man slowly dwindle from lover of life to bedridden body, with a mind still sharp enough to keep up with the financial markets.

While the reality of his condition was smack in front of me, I was in denial. No one wants to admit someone they love is dying. And nothing prepares you for the moment when it happens. Hope springs eternal, yet when is too much hope a bad thing? I was now confronted with that reality as I spoke with Brigitte.

"Is everything all right?" I asked.

There was a long pause. "Your father has died." Her voice was firm and controlled.

"What?" I replied, my cerebral shock absorbers kicking in. This couldn't be true. "When did this happen?"

"A few hours ago. He went into a coma. Your father lay lifeless, with tubes forcing air into his lungs. I couldn't bear it. The doctor said there was nothing more he could do, so I chose to remove the life support. That's no way for a person to live." Behind the stoic voice, I felt her heartache.

"Brigitte, it was the right thing to do," I quickly said, knowing she needed to hear it. "He would have hated us had we kept him alive. I'm sorry you had to do this alone." Tears welled up in my eyes as the news sunk in. I felt sick to my stomach.

"Right now I'm numb, just numb and exhausted," she said.

"I love you. We will speak in the morning," I replied.

I still held the phone after Brigitte hung up. My husband finished locking the dead bolts on the front door and walked over to me. His loving eyes revealed great concern; he knew what happened. What does one say at a time like this?

"My father died," I said in disbelief. The words came out of my mouth, but I was not in acceptance of the news. I felt confused.

His arms reached out to me, but I could not receive them. My heart shut down like a crashed computer. The delicious meal from a few hours ago turned sour in my stomach. I put the white slim-line phone back into its cradle, walked into the bathroom, and threw up. I was already sick with grief.

My dad had been a pillar of strength and unwavering inspiration. He was my beacon, a light to which I was completely and wholeheartedly attached. Being defeated was not part of his constitution. In many ways and for many reasons, he was the impetus behind my life. I always wanted to make him proud of me. Deep admiration for him and for how he met the challenges that God set before him kept me wondering how I might respond to the crises he experienced. If I inherited even half his enthusiasm for life and his ability not to complain about the challenges, I'd be happy.

The pain in my heart felt like a stabbing knife. My eyes puffy and bloodshot from crying, I lay in bed feeling all alone and scared. My husband lay asleep next to me, but that night I was immune to the hypnotic rhythm of our breath, which usually opened the cosmic gate to dreamland. The sandman was nowhere nearby.

I began to remember stories told from family members about the early years that shaped the course of my father's life.

Peter's Courage

January 23, 1940, was such a cold day that children at a New York City school were dismissed minutes early. Since parents had not been notified of an early dismissal, they had not yet arrived to pick up their kids. Children ran and played around the schoolyard unattended. Three six-year-old boys stood on the corner, feeling like they had been let out of prison early. They were too busy laughing and horsing around to notice the oncoming sanitation truck that lost control, jumping the curb as it turned a hard right. The truck caught Peter's jacket and dragged him off the curb, pulling him under the massive vehicle. In seconds the little boy lay seemingly lifeless in pools of blood under the oversized machine, while children and teachers filled the air with screams and horror. The two other boys stood motionless, in shock, and had to be escorted away from the scene.

Peter spent a year in intensive care as doctors did their best to save his life. During surgery one thing was clear: An amputation was necessary. The question was whether they would be able to keep the kneecap. With little time to deliberate, they reached a unanimous decision to keep the kneecap. At the time, it seemed like the most humane choice. However, it would prove to be a painful decision that would plague Peter for decades.

Residents in the Italian neighborhood of East New York in Brooklyn came willingly and regularly to give donations of blood, which meant so much to my grandparents. As followers of the teachings of the Catholic Church, they soon forgave the truck driver, praying he might find some peace.

On occasion the truck driver would call to find out how Peter was. How does a person continue living while feeling responsible for an accident? Several years later, the family of the truck driver called my grandparents to inform them he had died. I can only guess it was of a broken heart.

Meanwhile, young Peter was like a war veteran, learning how

to walk with a prosthetic limb. After a year in intensive care and then years of continued rehabilitation, the time came for him to reintegrate himself into society. To attend school, he climbed into the small school bus for handicapped children. Classmates advanced to the next grade, but he was left behind to figure out how his life would be with one good leg and one bad leg. Many secondary health issues, such as infections, arose as a result of his injury. As a growing young boy, Peter learned how to cope with his new condition. By the time he turned fifteen, the onset of young adulthood had pushed him to learn how to take control of his body and his life.

Handball was the game of choice back then, and remarkably, despite nagging discomfort, he became an expert player. He hopped from one end of the court to the other, catching up with most of the balls that came swiftly in his direction and then slapping them back against the cement wall to score a point for his two-man team.

Baseball was his second love. With a strong swing of the bat, he would knock the ball past second base and run quickly around the bases with one good leg and one weak one. The good leg developed into a strong and muscular limb, providing excellent balance and coordination for certain sports. His friends were in awe, and he soon received well-deserved respect and admiration for his fortitude.

Strong determination for success drove him to fine-tune his mid-framed body to resemble a professional bodybuilder's through weight lifting, chin-ups, and push-ups. With six-pack abs and bulging biceps, women were naturally attracted to him. He combed his dark brown, wavy hair into a semi-long pompadour, similar to Hollywood movie stars. Add in his big brown eyes with eyelashes that are every woman's dream, fully defined lips, and a warm smile, he exuded sexy, good looks.

God gave him innate charm and confidence. He drew on that to put himself through two years of college, which was uncommon in those days. He landed a job in the banking industry, and that brought many other opportunities to advance his career in years to come.

Feeling like a victim was never part of his outlook. My aunt bragged about her brother: "Your father never complained about anything; he just kept going. I don't know how he did it, but he did. He was a likeable guy, and the girls loved him just the same!"

At around age twenty, Peter met Mary, a pretty girl from Prospect Heights. Her long, curly brown hair and Mediterranean almond-shaped eyes caught his attention from across the bar at the local bowling alley one Saturday night.

Mary was six months older than he and worked in a factory as a seamstress. Her father had passed away from cancer when she was sixteen years old, forcing her to leave school and go to work to help support the family. After two years of courtship, they were married and became parents to three children. I was firstborn.

After seventeen years of marriage, my parents divorced. They were once Soul Mates. Unable to resolve their relationship issues, they chose to separate. Several years later, they met new partners and both remarried. At fifteen years old, I observed how happy they were with new partners. While most children are distraught by divorce, I was at peace with it. They seemed happier and managed to reinvent their relationship for the sake of their three children. My parents and stepparents became good friends and often dined out together, without the children. Most people didn't understand this kind of relationship. It was progressive in those days, but I was proud to have four open-minded parents. I loved them all very deeply and considered myself extremely lucky to have four wonderful role models. Christmas festivities were joyful, filled with laughter, and lots of food!

Traveling was my dad's favorite pastime with his new wife, Brigitte, a senior stewardess for Trans World Airlines. I was inspired by them both to travel and see the world. In his early forties, another surgery would be needed to remove the troublesome kneecap, which finally ended the physical pain he had endured since the accident.

More than life itself, he loved his family and children. He was my rock. Now he was gone, and I was lost.

The Promise

Two years before I came home to that fateful phone call, my father was diagnosed with colon cancer. The initial news shocked the family. My heart pounded in fear when I first heard it as bewilderment set in. Dad was only fifty-one and disheartened by the diagnosis. He was a proud man but not so proud as to hold back his emotions. At times he was choked up talking about his condition. "I don't think I will live a long life," Dad would often say. The family would become angry when hearing these words and tell him to stop thinking these thoughts. He was afraid, and so was I.

He and Brigitte immediately sought help from the Macrobiotic Institute in New York City, and changed their diet to build a strong immune system while following a traditional treatment of chemotherapy. Dad would often express doubt that he could be cancer-free despite trying to cure himself through natural methods and macrobiotic foods. He'd shake his head, look down at the ground, and say, "I don't know. I just don't know." I suppose his own intuition of the future was clear to him, but not to the rest of the family.

Cancer had spread throughout the perineum. Doctors gave him six months to two years to live. I cherished the close father-daughter relationship we had, and now I wasn't sure how to live without him. Oddly, I felt an urge to pray to God.

A few days later, I was back at work. I loved my job in commercial real estate in New York City. After a corporate management meeting in an uptown building I had been to dozens of times, I exited to notice a small church directly across the street. Somehow, I had never seen it before. But now, there it was, suddenly right in my line of sight as if to extend an invitation to come in. I looked around. It was a bright, sunny day on Madison Avenue, which was always bustling with people, cars, and honking cabbies. That church drew my attention as if nothing else was happening. The moment seemed just right for going inside. I was hesitant but then walked up the steps and entered the sacred space.

The heavy wooden door closed behind me and instantly blocked out the noise from the street. The silence was intimidating and unfamiliar. I felt uneasy, but why? Why did I feel uncomfortable in the house of God? Scanning the small number of pews, I saw only a few people praying with bowed heads. For a moment I wondered, *Why are they here, praying for something, hoping for something? Why do we seek God's help only when we're in pain?*

My breath became shallow. I glanced up at the ornate altar surrounded by colorful stained-glass windows. A hint of frankincense lingered in the musty air. Statues of the holy ones held strategic positions throughout the church so that with every turn of my head, one of them was staring at me with open arms. There was no escaping now. Was I worthy enough to be in such a sacred place? My Roman Catholic upbringing had not escaped me, but recalling my failure to maintain the teachings of the Church stirred old lingering guilt.

An empty dark wood pew in the middle of the church looked appropriate—not too close, not too far away from the altar. I tiptoed toward it, scooted into the center, and knelt. The wooden knee-rest was without padding and uncomfortable, but the moment I began to pray, the discomfort faded away. Chin to chest, hands clasped with rosary beads draped around pointed fingers, my hands recollected the sign of the cross.

"In the name of the Father, the Son, and the Holy Spirit. Dear God, I want to ask You to cure the cancer in my father's body, but that feels unrealistic. I don't know why it feels unrealistic, but it does. Do I doubt You? Do I even know You? You can heal everything, and if it's possible, please heal him. I fear You are calling him home, but what about me? What am I supposed to do? Who will take care of me? I can't tell You what to do, but please, give me the maximum amount of time possible before You take him. Please God, hear me, and I will do whatever You ask."

My prayers were answered. My father died exactly two years later, giving me the great gift of the maximum amount of time to spend with him. I called him daily, spent every weekend creating memories. Yes, I bargained with God. The Almighty remembered my promise that I would do whatever He asked, and held me to it. It wasn't yet time, but I, too, would be called home—not through physical death, but through an awakening that would change the way I lived, how I viewed life, and provide a spiritual understanding of who I am and why I existed on Earth now.

Conclusion: Every negative, hurtful, challenging situation has a silver lining. Therein is the awakening. You are never alone or abandoned by a God who loves you deeply and wants to give you everything you desire. Look upward.

Chapter 2

She's Come Undone

After my father's death, I often felt confused and disoriented as uncontrollable thoughts bombarded my mind. Who or what would fill the empty space within me now? Who would I depend on? A piece of me had died. The grief was deep and the pain unrelenting as the relationship cords once connected to my beacon of light dangled in midair, attached to nothing. The connection between father and daughter had been one of my great joys, and now it was gone.

Feeling alone, I began to distance myself from the marriage. Something had changed within me, which was unexplainable. I felt uneasy and restless. The things that once brought me joy were no longer of interest. As much as I tried to get myself back to the "old" me, before my father's passing, it was not happening.

I remembered a festive wedding my family attended six years earlier. We danced the night away with friends and strangers, sipping on the finest French champagne. My strapless, red-taffeta cocktail dress was enhanced by the glitter of diamond earrings and a matching pendant. The open-toed red pumps finished a "lady in red" look.

My father extended his hand to me and asked, "Shall we dance?" He took the lead to Frank Sinatra's "Summer Wind."

"You are my shining star," he whispered. Without a care in the world, we circled the dance floor with the slow-slow-quick-quick pace of the dance.

At that moment life was good, joyous, filled with love. But now, the joy of life was gone.

Weekly visits to his grave bestowed little comfort. Each time I placed fresh flowers at the headstone engraved with "Beloved father and husband," I hoped this was a dream, and I'd snap out of it. The quiet resting place was small but beautifully landscaped. A peaceful aura surrounded each headstone. Was he at peace sleeping alone six feet under the earth? I certainly was not at peace being alive. The scent of red carnations satisfied my senses for a moment, but then remembering why I was there, triggered another cycle of grief. The strength drained out of my body like passing through a wide-open portal through the uncontrollable flow of salty tears.

Grief is known to trigger old wounds and cause emotional, mental, and physical disturbances. It cracks open the wall around your heart, letting pain from the past rush forward like a river without a dam. Coping with his death during the day was difficult. Nights were worse. Old wounds slowly began to surface in the still of the night. My physical body grew tired and my mind weary from confusion and lack of sleep.

One day while I was placing a fresh bunch of daisies at his grave, a crazy thought brushed over me. It came out of nowhere. Darkness was my new companion, and I felt the grief was honestly more about me than him. Living now in the light and love of God, wouldn't he be whole and at peace? Believing in the afterlife was part of my consciousness. Could the grief be about poor me and all the difficult life-circumstances that haunted me from childhood to this very moment? This realization brought a whole new light to the subject of his death and crisis. If my grief was about me, then what would I need to do about it? I needed to run away, run somewhere, anywhere to get away from myself, my thoughts, and my life. How do these abstract thoughts find their way into our minds?

Kentucky-Style Genetics

Two months later an urge to visit my younger sister and her boyfriend swept over me. I needed a dose of serenity because everything about life at the time was overwhelming. I purchased a round-trip ticket from New York to Kentucky and told my husband I'd be back on Sunday evening. Exhausted, I dragged my tired body to the airport, and off I flew to Kentucky in hope of getting some guidance, an answer, or just some comfort away from my life.

They were horse people who both worked at the racetrack. He was a trainer, my sister a would-be jockey. I was ceaselessly impressed with their abilities to handle these large, majestic creatures. Honestly, I was terrified of horses.

A big white and red Ford Bronco pulled up to the outdoor arrival area at Lexington's Blue Grass Airport to pick up a lost Soul. The step up to get into the darn vehicle was so high I could barely lift my leg enough to get in. After all, New York girls are used to driving in sports cars, and taxicabs. Who knew such a monstrous truck existed?

"How ya doin', Pauline?" asked the boyfriend with his southern drawl. His sandy-blond hair was windblown from the open windows. "Your sister's still workin', so I'm here to git ya."

"Not bad, not bad," I replied. It was a hot summer day, and I realized the big machine he was driving didn't have air-conditioning. I was out of my comfort zone and not happy about it. Who ever heard of a vehicle without air-conditioning?

Despite my discomfort, I appreciated the beauty of the landscape. Perhaps I was beginning to stop and smell the roses. Every rolling hill and mountain was covered with the most beautiful greenish-blue hue. I finally understood why Kentucky is called the "Bluegrass

State." The air was fresh and clean, the lifestyle calm, though maybe a little slow from a New Yorker's point of view. Could I ever get used to such a simple lifestyle?

We drove to the motel they were living in at the time, making idle conversation. He wore dingy jeans covered in dust and grime from the racetrack. I wore my usual black slim-leg travel pants with matching jacket and one-inch stacked heels. And I wondered if he thought I was the stuffiest person he'd ever met!

Seeing my sister for the first time since Dad died stirred more emotions. Two sisters from the same family were living completely different lives while experiencing different reactions to Dad's passing. She seemed okay; I was not. I noticed she still had the stylish black-leather shoe-boots I gave her for Christmas a few years ago. She would often remind me how much she loved them. I was delighted that she retained a piece of her New York style in horse country.

Working at the racetrack required full days on both Saturday and Sunday. The next morning they left at six o'clock, giving me a lot of time to sit alone in the tiny rented room, thinking and sorting out my life. Only one small window let sunlight in the darkly paneled chamber. A small loveseat opened up to sleep one person—me. Across the room was a queen bed in which they slept. Oh yes, and one small chair for Sam, the dog. Looking around the room, I wondered, *What in the world am I doing here? What am I running away from? What pearls of wisdom would Kentucky give me that New York could not?*

The new environment did not change my relationship with my nighttime friend, insomnia, nor my nagging fatigue. Each night I lay awake listening to the soulful sound of a symphony of snores orchestrated by three other bodies in the room. I fantasized about what it might be like to fall into a deep REM sleep. I fantasized about what it might be like to wake up feeling refreshed.

We spent two evenings together, talking and dining in local restaurants that were as simple as the lifestyle. I indulged in southern fried chicken—comfort food, as they say. My sister had just experienced the same loss I did, yet she could still smile. I could not.

Falling Apples—Sweet, Sour, Salty

The big yellow Lab and I sat for two days staring at each other or watching TV, him on the chair, me on the bed. Years prior, I often thought about writing down the positive and negative aspects of my relationships with boyfriends as a way to figure out if it was worth investing my time. I never actually did it because it seemed harsh, maybe even a little silly. But then a weird urge came over me. I thought about my parents. Could I actually be silly enough to write down the polar opposite traits of my parents? I grabbed a sheet of lined paper and drew four columns. Two columns were for Mom and two columns were for Dad. On the top of Mom's two columns I wrote "Sweet/Sour" and did the same for Dad. On the bottom was a section titled "Salt," which included other traits from both sets of grandparents. This was not about a boyfriend or husband any longer; it was about my genetics! What personality characteristics did I inherit from my parents and grandparents? Curious and excited to fill in the blanks, I jotted down first impressions.

At first I was selective about which characteristics I had unquestionably inherited. In the Sweet column under my mother, I wrote the word "strength," and in Dad's column, "courage." In the Sour column under Mom I wrote "strict" and in Dad's, "materialistic."

Remembering my grandparents, who were all deceased, I wrote "stubborn/wise," "silly/giving," and, "ignorant/hardworking" in the Salt section. It was easier to describe my grandparents without guilt as they lay in the love and peace of God's Universe. Describing my parents was more difficult as three of them remained alive and well.

Continued blasts of inspiration swept through me as more genetic traits showed up: "insecure/loving, judgmental/compassionate, arrogant/easygoing, serious/funny, quiet/talkative, generous/

spoiled, hardheaded/understanding, demanding/open-minded, defensive/honest, stupid/smart, abusive/steadfast, shabby/classy, superior/inferior, introverted/extroverted, fearful/fearless, strong/ weak, bullying/passive, charming/gruff." Writing the list of mirrored patterns, I felt twinges of energy in unusual places in my body. Carefully choosing only the ones I was willing to acknowledge, suddenly came a burst of laughter and tears. Who was I kidding? It was all too funny and all too scary to fathom. A revelation had been exposed.

The apples didn't fall far from the tree! I was now looking at myself in the mirror of my parents and grandparents. I now saw in myself every trait that my parents and grandparents had, though I had never been aware of it. Humility, I understood, could be my greatest teacher as it was vital to recognize my own weaknesses and shortcomings. At the same time, I thanked God for my strengths as they would be the source from which I would heal the parts of myself that weren't.

All of it was mine. Yes, all the sweet, the sour, and the salty had genetically manifested as the person now trying to find herself, lying on a bed in a tiny motel room in Kentucky. *Can this be true?* I wondered. *Can all this be really true?* Yes, it was all so frightfully yet honestly true.

What I did not know at the time and learned much later was acknowledging opposite energies, such as superior/inferior, actually helps balance and strengthen the middle ground, which in this case would be healthy self-esteem or nonjudgment. Looking at both sides of the coin is necessary to heal and balance the mind, body, and Soul.

An hour passed after this exercise downloaded into my foggy yet receptive mind. I lay immobilized on the bed as my left brain attempted to sort out the logic behind this brilliant idea. Okay, so what? Acknowledgment is half the battle, right? There was something viable to work with now, yet I felt stupid for engaging in the exercise. Again I wondered, *Where do crazy ideas like this come from?* I turned the television back on and slipped into mindlessness.

At 5:00 p.m. the sound of keys jangling in the door caught my attention. Folding the paper into quarters, I quickly stashed it into the side zipper of my purse to hide all evidence of the newly revealed information. My sister and her beau walked in, a whiff of horse sweat following them. It wasn't bad; I actually liked it. Somehow the primal scent grounded me back into my body. After such a brilliant experience, I wanted to crawl under covers and go to sleep in total humility.

"So what did you do today, Paul?" my sister asked, using her lifelong nickname for me.

"Nothing. Sam and I watched TV and read some magazines."

On Sunday the big white and red Ford Bronco returned me to Blue Grass Airport. The ride was just as bumpy, hot, and uncomfortable as two days ago, but somehow it bothered me less. As I sat in the back seat listening to my sister and boyfriend talk horse talk, my hair blew around in every direction possible, symbolic of how my life was unfolding. Oddly, I didn't care and felt a degree of freedom from the rigidity I had flown in with. Searching for some great pearls of wisdom from this trip, I remembered the folded paper labeled "Sweet, Sour, and Salty," which deserved further examination on returning home.

From time to time I added more words to the "Sweet, Sour, Salty" worksheet. Slowly, the worksheet filled up with a list of adjectives describing the people who consciously, unconsciously, and genetically shaped my personality and life.

So if this is who I am, then what did I need to do about it?

Socrates Speaks

"The unexamined life is not worth living," taught the Greek philosopher Socrates. As uncertainty prevailed, my mind wandered back to 1977, when I attended Franklin College, an American school in Lugano, Switzerland. Enrollees from around the world comprised the student body. I was privileged to be able to study abroad, be exposed to diversity at a young age, and to travel to various countries.

Attending a foreign school had been my idea. Shortly after graduating high school, I felt an urge to seek colleges abroad and expressed this to my parents. I don't know why that was. Brigitte, being a native of Germany, felt this would be an exceptional experience for me to mature.

One weekend I called the international operator to obtain contact information for various American colleges in Europe. After reviewing several options, I felt the school in Switzerland was the right one.

I called Brigitte, excited to tell her the news. "I think I've found just the right school for me. It's in Lugano, Switzerland, and sounds wonderful. It's a two-year program."

Brigitte replied, "Switzerland! That's interesting. I just met the president of Franklin College in Switzerland on a flight to Italy."

"Oh my God! Yes, that's the name of the school I discovered too!" We were astounded by the coincidence, or we may say there are no such things as coincidences. I applied immediately.

At Franklin, students were able to choose two weeks of academic travel to select countries every semester. Once, I chose to go to Greece. While in Athens, our group of twenty students, guided by our teacher, visited many tourist attractions. One site is now finding its way back into my conscious mind. It's a sacred place in the city of Athens.

On the day of our tour, a hot sun hid behind thick clouds, but the temperature was pleasant. The dusty roads in the ancient city made travel by foot challenging. I was grateful for the clouds as walking in the sun all day would have drained the life out of us. We arrived at our destination, which had marble steps leading up to a courtyard surrounded by green shrubbery. White-marble benches formed a U-shape in which men had sat and meditated in ancient times. Outside the walls of greenery of this sacred place was the usual business of the city. But within the walls lived an entirely different energy. It was quiet, peaceful—almost as if this small spot were a serene island all to itself within a busy city. One particular spot on the bench had been filed down to accommodate sitting buttocks.

"It is proclaimed that Socrates sat in this very spot and meditated for hours at a time," explained our teacher and guide.

In that moment, something unexplainable was triggered. Completely intrigued and fascinated by that spot, my attention remained glued to it. After several minutes of historical explanation, our group walked out of the courtyard. Hoping not to be noticed, I ran over to Socrates's seat and sat in it for a moment. There was no logical explanation why the urge to sit in this one spot overcame me, but I succumbed to it.

Sitting with eyes closed, waiting to experience something extraordinary in that moment, and ... nothing happened. Slightly disappointed but then dismissing the validity of this urge, I ran to catch up to the group en route to the next historical site.

Something about that moment from my college years haunted me later as the yearning for wholeness was unknowingly stealing my heart from my second marriage. The vision of my young self, sitting in the philosopher's seat, came rushing forward with a clear message: It was time to self-examine and deal with the unseen darkness that was steering my ship. To see the truth would not be pretty or easy, but to deny it would be to remain in an unending cycle of destruction. The darkness needed my attention for it longed to be seen, heard, and healed. Nothing about my life seemed normal.

Why, at age thirty, was I experiencing so much drama when most of my friends were married with young children? I felt like an outcast, still trying to find myself at a time when I was supposed to be settled down, creating a family, just like everyone else. I checked in to that old familiar place, therapy.

It was time to examine deeply and reflect on myself and my life. Eleven years after that moment in Athens, Socrates had spoken.

The Examination Begins

When I walked into the lobby of the building where my former therapist conducted her sessions, an elevator door was open as if waiting for my arrival. I stepped inside and was transported to the sixteenth floor. It took no effort to remember the way to the "office of tears." It had been a long while since I had needed the help of a professional, but as I approached the door to the waiting room, which was slightly ajar, a feeling of relief swept over me. Help was on the way. I peeked in to see how many strangers were waiting for their sessions of tears to start. Thankfully, the room was empty. Classical music playing softly in the background soothed my over-energized brain.

"Come in, Pauline." Oh yes, I remembered it well. The office of tears was about to become my home for a short while.

Forming a sort of semicircle, two tan rounded-wicker chairs were on the far side of the room, and near the window was one straight-backed chair against the wall, in which the therapist sat. The chair closest to the door was my best choice in case I needed to cut the session short and run away from myself. As I snuggled my body into the dark-blue plush cushions, I felt safe.

We sat in silence for a few moments. That felt uncomfortable. She would sit for the entire forty-five-minute session without saying a word if need be, waiting for the client to begin. She remained quiet, looking down at the white shag rug, waiting for a word, any word, to find its way out of my mouth. Her outfit was stylish, as always in the latest fashion, and her beautiful pink angora sweater caught my eye. *Stop paying attention to her clothing and start talking, Pauline!* Oh, my mind was spinning like a top.

"I think I need to be alone," I finally began, "by myself to find something, but I'm not sure what it is."

Her eyes rolled up to make direct contact with mine. "You don't seem like the kind of person who should be alone or really wants to be alone. So what's this all about?" Her voice was even-toned yet comforting.

I began my woeful story of how my father died and how my current marriage was in trouble since my heart crashed after receiving the news. "Why is my life like this?" I asked. "What's wrong with me? How many times am I going to get married before I'm happy?"

"Well, Pauline, you are in crisis again. Don't be so hard on yourself. And you'll get married as many times as you need to in order to get it right." She was familiar with the circumstances of the first divorce.

I stared at her with wide-open eyes. I wondered, *Is she crazy?* What kind of statement was that? And yet such beautiful words from her lips were reassuring. I might not be senseless after all, and someone in the Universe understood the pending insanity without judgment.

"But we need to look at some patterns," she continued.

I thought about the Sweet, Sour, Salty worksheet stashed away in my dresser drawer. My stomach tied itself into a knot as I sank deeper into the blue cushions. I grabbed a handful of tissues. The roller-coaster ride was about to begin. And so the journey of a lifetime was set in motion with a crisis that sent me into an unexplored place within—my dark side, my wounds, my fears, my strengths.

The office of tears lived up to its reputation as I recalled the hurtful memories etched in my heart. I was still grieving the divorce from five years ago, now mourning my father's death, and facing a mysterious presence guiding me into an unknown future.

"Why did I get divorced the first time?" I asked. "What went wrong?"

She spoke softly. "Let's look at what *you* could have done differently."

I didn't like that response, but it was the only answer. I had to look at me and only me, my patterns of behavior in relationship. Could I have been softer, more easygoing, and less rigid?

"Why can't my second marriage support me through a difficult time?" I asked.

Again she answered by returning the responsibility of the situation to me. "What's inside of *you*, Pauline? What's trying to come out?"

"I don't know. I can't explain it. But something is happening, and I can't control it." Tears welled up in my eyes. I tried as hard as I could to refrain from showing emotion, but I couldn't control myself. Something unknown and uncontrollable was surfacing, pushing through the darkness like a bulldozer.

"Don't worry, Pauline. You will be okay," she said with a gentle smile.

Sometimes just hearing someone else say you'll be fine brings comfort.

My crises were about me and no one else. It was time to look directly at these questions and seek the answers, no matter how painful. Years prior, therapy offered support as I went through a divorce. Now it seemed therapy was offering something deeper, and more personally transformational. Feelings, emotions, and thoughts surrounding the past were deeply buried while I was unaware they still existed. Beginning to see the errors of my ways was challenging but very necessary. To take responsibility for my life meant I had to stop blaming anyone or anything for the way in which my life was unfolding and for the way I felt about myself. My sole responsibility was to heal myself and my life. With great difficulty I started to learn how to take responsibility for my part in every situation and look no further than my own behavior. The behavior of others was beyond my control. Personal examination became the theme of that year. What I didn't know was that it would become a staple for the rest of my life—not in traditional therapy, but through spiritual growth and awakening.

Upholding the Promise

My husband was an extraordinary man, but I was inconsolable. He couldn't take my father's place; no one could. Together we had created a good life with promising careers in real estate. His in small building sales, mine in commercial management. We talked about buying a home and having children, living a traditional life with family nearby. Naturally I would be a stay-at-home mom just like my mother.

The future had appeared promising and full of joy. But something huge was missing now, and I needed to find it. The fine lifestyle that we once thrived on left me feeling empty and hungry for something more fulfilling. Time passed, and the void grew deeper. Something that I depended on my father for was now missing. The quest to find it prevailed.

The path of my life was changing without my conscious permission. A mysterious presence was imparting messages into my mind. Feelings and thoughts seemingly from outer space came plummeting in, proposing that what I needed was to be alone to find out who Pauline actually was.

One evening as I did the laundry, I wondered what direction my life was going in when a feeling of freedom swept over me. All of a sudden I felt totally free and joyful. Then the feeling vanished as quickly as it came, returning me to the present moment as I placed wet clothes into the dryer.

On another occasion, while driving I fantasized about making some kind of positive difference in the world, maybe speaking or teaching. Instantly feelings of insecurity surfaced. *Oh, not me, I'm just an ordinary person.* As I drove an image in my mind's eye of a parent holding the hand of a child appeared. The image was so powerful it took my breath away. I pulled the car over to the curb and parked for several minutes as I processed the image wondering what it meant. I later learned the image represented me as the child, and God as the parent. The image transmitted a wave of energy to me in that moment which caused slight confusion, yet there was an underlying feeling of excitement. Connection with the divine was slowly happening. I was being shown the way forward.

The revelation to be alone and feel free or purposeful seemed on one level as stupid as eating rocks. Yet the truth of it was too strong to ignore, despite my fears. Divine guidance gently revealed that another divorce was required to find my self. I needed to seek the help of God. I tried to suppress these irrational thoughts but was unable to. They kept sweeping over me like an ocean wave over which I had no control.

My second husband was a true angel who had helped me overcome the painful circumstances of my first divorce. Unconditionally, he provided a haven in which I might release a hurtful past through his love and kindness. His adoration and gentle nature helped me regain my strength and self-esteem from the first marriage. Our relationship provided a safety net, a place to be nurtured and to feel worthy again. I admired his nonjudgmental attitude toward people, and surely I'd learned a few good things from him in the course of our life together. He'd be a great dad. Isn't this what we long for? Wouldn't this be enough?

The messages from outer space, as it seemed, were overriding any logical thoughts or traditional visions I had about the future. It was pulling me out of my safety net, and I hated it. I hated these thoughts! It killed me to think that our marriage could not sustain my darkest hour. But a volcano was erupting inside me, and the death of my father was what stirred it into activity. Shortly after my trip to Kentucky and then through therapy, the marriage began to crumble. I allowed the situation to run its own course without any explanation to my husband or my family. We argued a lot, yet I made little attempt to reconcile. I became disinterested in the things we had once dreamed about.

"There's a new house on the market. Would you like to go and see it?" my husband asked. "It's near your mom."

"Not really," I said, annoyed by his question.

"What's wrong, Pauline?"

I didn't answer. I had no words to describe what I was feeling. I walked away, leaving him in the living room frustrated and hurt. I stormed into the bathroom, slammed the door, collapsed my face into my hands, and sobbed. I didn't understand why I had not been able to restart the crashed computer in my heart. My loving heart remained shut down and broken. What in the world was happening? What was he going through? Feeling helpless and powerless, the focus now was on my life. Selfishly, all I knew was my grief.

Again and again I wondered, *Why is my life like this? What's wrong with me?* I believed I was a good person who was honest, ethical, and generous. I was raised to always try to do the right thing by others. None of this seemed to matter anymore. Nothing seemed to make any sense. My yearning for wholeness grew strong. There was no place else to look except inward. God was guiding my life, upholding my part of the bargain agreement established years prior that I would do whatever He asked of me for giving the maximum time with Dad before taking him home. Apparently I was being asked to find my true self in communion with the Universe, and that required being alone for a while.

One year after my father's death, a second divorce was pending.

The Remembrance

Before my father died, I never looked deeply at life or death because I felt no reason to. When things were good, I expected they would stay that way and took them for granted. Don't we all? Everything seemed to be working well, so why try to fix something that wasn't broken? As long as Dad was alive and I was married, life was good. There was no reason to examine anything. But the second divorce took its toll. My state of mind was confused and weary, which forced me to look at life, death, and God.

Family and friends didn't understand why my life was unfolding in a nontraditional way. Nor did I. Life was simply happening as if it had a mind of its own. Very few people I had depended on gave me the support I needed. And many didn't hesitate to express their disapproval. Disheartening as that was, it provided the greatest opportunity to learn how to be true to myself and own my power.

When the true path of awakening finds you, it is common for family members and close friends to criticize or attempt to dissuade you. An awakening will not look like the traditional life. This path can seem irrational to those who are not ready to awaken. As a result, you may find the people you have previously depended on to support you acting in hurtful ways by not supporting you. Why? Because if you change, they will be challenged to change, and that is fearful. Most people prefer to stay in a comfort zone of non-growth. Your empowerment comes from internal growth, and not needing anyone's approval.

As I grappled with this lack of support, a chapter from the first self-help book I read at sixteen years old sparked a remembrance. "You don't need their approval," said the late Dr. Wayne Dyer from his brilliant book, *Your Erroneous Zones.*

Ah, a revelation! I didn't need the approval of anyone but myself. No one knew me or what I needed to do better than I did. I began following inner guidance, even when the guidance seemed illogical and drastic. The guidance was not strong; it was faint but present. Trusting and understanding were the challenge.

During the next several years I searched for something intangible as my yearning for wholeness grew strong. Therapy helped, but it wasn't enough. I partied several nights a week. Manhattan is the city that never sleeps, with bars, restaurants, and meeting places seemingly inviting me in to distract me from myself. A few glasses of wine with friends after work at happy hour became a habit during the week. Dance clubs were a better choice on the weekend, thinking that I would find what I was searching for outside myself. Yet each time I felt enjoyment from the outer world, the next morning I'd wake up feeling empty. I began to see how addiction is formed through trying continuously to fill ourselves with things that satisfy temporarily, and then leave us needing to engage them over and over to fill the emptiness or numb the pain. It doesn't work. It seems when we are in crisis or hurting in some way, our first reactions are to distract ourselves from the pain we feel. I believe this is a poor coping mechanism as it creates more disharmony.

Before long my health severely declined. The impact of the losses was too great. Experiencing two divorces and the death of my father within five years, I was emotionally depleted, physically ill, and spiritually empty.

Paulo, a colleague from work, noticed that my father's death shook me to the core and gave me a book. "I think this will help you," he said. His smile was unusually confident.

Paulo was a kind man with a gentle spirit. He possessed a unique intuitive knowing about life but was never eager to discuss it. *The Seth Material,* by Jane Roberts, reminded me that spirit is eternal; only the body is shed upon death.

Believing in spirits and the afterlife was not new to me. From the age of sixteen, I dabbled in tarot cards, Ouija boards, and séances, and I sought the advice of spiritual counselors and psychics rather than my parents. I must have needed a reminder of the metaphysical concepts that were innately part of my perception about life before the material world took over. Why had I forgotten such an important part of human existence? Could it have been the focus on material accumulation and lifestyle that rerouted my spirit toward a less-fulfilling direction? I believe so.

Reading the self-help book reminded me that although a person has gone into the afterlife, a loving connection can be maintained. Many stories in the book jolted a remembrance of how eternal the Soul is and how our deceased loved ones are not departed. Rather, their forms have changed, and they remain connected to us. Our job is to reach upward and connect with them. Hope was renewed.

Shortly thereafter, the connection kicked in. I routinely returned home from a day's work and collapsed from exhaustion. I could often feel the spirit of my father in my safe haven, and welcomed its peaceful, loving energy. One night while sitting on the living room couch, there was a moment of clarity. It was a weeknight. A few dishes remained in the sink unwashed. I was too tired to clean up. Erratic thoughts had their way with me in my weakened condition, crying for my father, crying for me, beating myself up about my first husband, about my second husband.

> *Then, for what seemed like only a moment, the outside world completely disappeared as my thoughts spiraled downward into self-hatred. All was quiet—with the exception of the racket going on in my head. Why, why, why is my life like this? I'm such a pathetic outcast. Who lives like this?*
>
> *My eyes closed, and all I saw was blackness. And then it hit me. This is exactly where I need to be. Dad's death is part of a grander plan. It gives me the impetus to explore the unknown mystery of life. I am living a scripted and necessary experience. This is my destiny, and nothing could have prevented it. My dependence on him was prohibiting me from living an authentic life true to me. To feel loved and accepted, I had conformed to commonly accepted behaviors that didn't really ring true for me. I no longer need to gain approval from my parents and others. I can live my own true life.*

Quickly coming back from the altered state, I dismissed these thoughts as irrational and stupid. They scared me so much I thought, *I must be out of my mind to think such horrid things. What kind of monster am I?* But the thoughts stayed with me, and soon I felt some degree of acceptance that his death, and the divorce was not only timely, it was indeed right on course with a divine plan unfolding, none of which I had any control over.

Dad would often say he would die young, and at age fifty-three, his prophecy was fulfilled. The new knowing I had about his death came from a greater source, something outside the human realm of understanding. And one thing was certain, it was undeniably true. My father was an intuitive man, and after this experience, my intuition awakened on an elementary level. His loving spirit imparted the intuitive gifts he used during his lifetime to his eldest daughter that night.

Healing the Past

Steered by this mysterious presence, I felt the urge to go back and heal past circumstances, including the relationship with my first husband and a friendship with my girlfriend, Rosalie.

Remembering the horrible and humiliating circumstances of the first divorce, I hesitated to contact him. What could possibly be discussed or resolved? What benefit could come from making contact after five years? Surely it would be disastrous to reach out and say that my deceased father or a mysterious presence was guiding me to heal my past. But once again, the urge from within was too strong to ignore. Visons of the ending of our marriage creeped into my mind's eye.

Back then I had called my father in fear, telling him I was afraid to remain in the home due to my husband's strange, abusive behavior. He instructed me to grab a few important items and leave the house. Following his guidance, I drove to my mother's home thirty minutes away.

Divorce proceedings began. The legal process was humiliating as I was deposed and interrogated by an attorney about what happened and how quickly—out of nowhere—the relationship disintegrated. I cringed as I recalled being spit at and verbally abused.

Months later I was legally permitted to return to the home to gather the rest of my belongings. On arriving there with my mom, my friend Rosalie, and the moving men, I saw that my belongings were strewn on the front lawn. Some furniture, clothing, and household items were piled up in one big ball. Walking over to the mess, I felt demeaned and wondered, *Why did he do this? What did I do to deserve this?*

One of the moving men walked over to me. "I've never seen anything like this." He scratched his head and then shook it back and forth.

With difficulty, I spoke in fragments. "Oh God, what do I? I mean how do I … Why would he … do about this?" My mind spiraled into confusion.

"This guy is a real jerk. Don't worry, we'll take care of everything." He placed his hand on my shoulder.

I held back tears and fought showing any emotion.

Then out of the patio door, a woman pranced onto the deck. Spiraling deeper into shock, I recognized her as one of the students who attended my aerobic classes. I had a small business teaching aerobics; a popular form of exercise at that time. She was friends with my husband and his brother. She seemed quite confident that she belonged in the home and I did not. I became nauseated and filled with anxiety. My husband had been cheating.

Returning to the present moment, I wondered, *Why now would I need to confront such an old wound?*

Despite the hurtful memory I mustered up enough courage and called him. I held my breath and dialed as my fingers automatically recalled his office number. To my surprise he answered the phone and was very receptive to my call. He agreed to meeting to discuss our long-ago failed marriage. I was shocked.

We met several times and discussed our history together. With an unfamiliar effort in communication, we admitted our personal contributions to the failure of the marriage. I admitted being too controlling, directing the way in which we lived, how to celebrate holidays, and creating what I thought was a good life. He apologized for not being present enough to communicate his feelings, resulting in his own resentment of the marriage causing him to be abusive. I believe the root of the hurtful circumstances was insecurity and immaturity on both sides. The ease with which we now discussed these issues was astonishing. The love we shared was still present. Our eyes met often as we talked, and love was expressed through our karmic attraction. But destiny would continue to move us in separate directions.

Never did I think to go back into my past until the inner urge was present. The past is gone, so why go back? While the past might be over, the energy of all circumstances can remain locked inside. I became aware that my father, and perhaps divine spirits, were pointing the way forward. In much awe, curiously and cautiously I began to pay attention to and trust the unseen guidance. The energy was given from above for us to meet, discuss, and heal the past. And so it was done. Healing the disaster of my first marriage enabled me to move onward. At least now there was some resolution and peace about the past.

Not so coincidently, around this same time a male friend from my past called me to apologize for his horrible behavior. My mind drifted back in time.

The phone was ringing; it was my sister. "Hi, Paul. Listen, Candice just called to say she has a message for you. She wouldn't say what it was but stressed it was important, like urgent!" Candice was my sister's mother-in-law, who had psychic abilities. I had never met her in person.

"Candice wants to speak with me? I can't imagine why, but I'll call her immediately." I jotted down the number and dialed it quickly.

"Hello, Candice. It's Pauline. I understand you have a message for me."

"Yeah, honey. Now listen up."

I did as she asked, trying to pay attention to every word dictated by a true southern drawl. "You know anything about psychics?" she asked.

"Oh, yes, Candice. I am familiar with them."

"Good, 'cause I got that dang ability. I been tryin' to get rid of it since I'm a teenager. Been askin' God to take this stupid thing from me, but He don't listen. I don't want this ability and been tryin' to avoid it forever. Now I'm sittin' here readin' magazines, and a damn spirit come into the room, and won't leave me alone. I put the TV on to ignore it, told it to go away, but it was persistent and wouldn't stop bothering me! I put the magazine down, turned off the TV, and yelled out, 'Who the hell are you, and what do you want?' Well, honey, it was your father. He wouldn't stop bothering me until I paid him some mind. He's concerned about you, said there's a male friend in your life who wants to harm you."

My stomach turned into knots. I had been getting midnight prank phone calls that caused sleepless nights and kept me on edge as I wondered who it could be and what they wanted.

"Do you have a male friend with light, sandy-colored hair? He's very fair-skinned and slightly overweight."

I swallowed hard. "Yes, I have such a friend."

"Well he wants to harm you. I see a slash across your face. He wants to maim your face, darlin', so you'll not be attractive to any other man. He loves you and is trying to keep you for himself."

I felt nauseated and light-headed. "Will he succeed in harming me? I've been getting prank calls in the midnight hours." My body trembled.

"He's got a plan, and it's him calling you, or he's got a friend helping him. He's trying to be your savior, so you'll fall in love with him."

"What kind of sick person would do such a thing?" I asked, upset and scared.

"Look, you just gotta end the friendship. He's got problems he don't tell you about. Git away from him, cut him off, and do it now. Don't wait 'cause he's got a plan."

"Thank you, Candice. I will get right on this. You've helped me, and I can't thank you enough. Do you realize how gifted you are?"

"Good. Git on it 'cause I don't want to have to use this dang ability again. I believe you will be fine, but don't wait one more minute, honey. Your father is around you."

"Yes, I know he is around me."

I ended the friendship with this man, never telling him about the psychic. Candice was right; it all made sense. A girlfriend stayed with me for a few weeks until the situation blew over.

I returned into the present moment, hearing his voice asking for my forgiveness. I found it difficult to forgive recollecting his manipulative, narcissistic behavior. But his admittance for the errors of his ways brought a sense of relief. I thanked him for calling and hung up the phone. Forgiveness felt too foreign a concept at this point, and his request for it was denied. My emotional state was still too fragile as I was trying to heal and sort out my life.

Rosalie

It had been many years since Rosalie and I spent time together. I smiled remembering how she and I used to sit under the stars in the wee hours of the morning after a few glasses of cheap white wine. We'd huddle together for hours on a dilapidated park bench and talk girl talk. Two young women in their early twenties, chatting the night away as if we had all the answers to all the world's problems.

The urge to contact Rosalie was present. There was no direct reason for the ending of our friendship, yet I felt a misunderstanding might have caused us to go our separate ways. I no longer knew where to find her, so I called her mother and left a message on the answering machine. I never received a return call, and for a while that bothered me. How was I to resolve the past without the cooperation of the other party? Why didn't she call me? I felt frustrated.

As time passed I realized the degree of control I had over such conditions was limited, even if the intention to resolve the past came from a good place. The only control I had was over myself. My heart spoke and concluded that I had given this situation my all, my best, and if it were not meant to be that we reconnect to resolve the past, I would have to be satisfied with my own efforts.

A year later I was sporting around in my Nissan hatchback and came to stop at a red light. As a car pulled up next to me, I glanced over at the driver and did a double-take. A woman with curly light-brown hair sat in the driver's seat. It was Rosalie! In the back seat her mother sat guarding a small child with curly hair, just like her mom. My friend looked content, as if life had treated her well. I felt a little jealous for what seemed to be her joy. Looking at the child brought up some thoughts that hadn't entered my mind in a long while. *Maybe having a child was my path to happiness?*

She was always an impatient driver and stared at the light, never noticing adjacent cars. The light turned green, and her dark-gray Chevy drove straight away while my vehicle turned a hard left, symbolizing that our lives were going in different directions. At that moment she drove out of my life ... literally.

Within moments my residual feelings from long ago vanished. All was resolved. Just like that. There was no logical explanation as to how it was resolved by this experience; it simply was! There were no words and no exchange of emotions between us. We were sitting side by side in our own cars, yet something happened on a nonphysical level that brought peace and resolution without words or confrontation. Although we would never speak again, the circumstances of the past seemed to fade away, leaving only a peaceful residue from which to move forward.

The world of nonphysical energy was presenting itself loud and clear. My mind was opening to higher thought patterns and ways of being as each new experience led the way. Some issues from the past were resolved in person; others were resolved at a nonphysical level. We do not work alone; nor are we ever alone. Spirit guides were working hard on my behalf, and the spirit guide I was in the process of attracting would soon reveal herself. What became clear was the need to strengthen my connection to spirit, so I began praying to God each night. In the most unusual way, the spirit world was becoming my guide, and I was spellbound by it.

The Human Messenger

In 1990 my health worsened. I was still exhausted and growing physically weaker. Getting up in the morning to go to work became strenuous. So did engaging in simple activities. My once perfect attendance record was tarnished with absenteeism and tardiness. I unintentionally lost weight, and clothes that once fit well were now baggy and hung down around my shoulders and hips. A once healthy olive complexion had a pasty pale-gray hue. The whites of my eyes appeared bloodshot from protruding red blood vessels. My almond-shaped eyes drooped down at the edges, forming a sad puppy-dog look. Bluish half circles outlined them and were visible through cosmetic cover-up. Feeling fatigued most of the time, I just wanted to sleep. But ironically, insomnia continued to be my new best friend in the darkness of night.

The simple pace of life was too much. My flesh and bones were screaming they could not go on. Doctors such as urologists, allergists, and internists couldn't find an illness despite performing numerous tests from various blood work to kidney scans and brain scans, and inserting all kinds of instruments into every orifice of my body. One visit to the ear, nose, and throat specialist stands out. I remember two ten-inch-long rods being inserted into my nasal passages. That was weird! Not one test provided a diagnosis as to what was causing the fatigue, chronic bronchitis, weakness, dark circles under my eyes, insomnia, digestive problems, or the inability to gain weight.

One day I was complaining to a coworker about my ailments. We were standing at the concierge desk in the lobby of the building I managed, greeting our tenants with a pleasant, "Good Morning." Several lobby walls were lined with squared windows, two feet by two feet, framed in light oak wood, allowing perfect observation of hurried New Yorkers.

The local mailman, John, came in and plopped his large sack of mail on the bench near us. Overhearing my complaints, he said, "Sounds like you have chronic fatigue syndrome."

"Chronic fatigue syndrome? What's that?" I asked.

"It's a condition you have when you're always tired and weak but you can't sleep. My girlfriend has it. That's how I know about it."

"That's God-awful, and it sounds like me! How do you get rid of it?" I questioned.

"Well, I'm not sure if you can, but I do know an excellent infectious disease doctor on the Upper East Side."

"Infectious disease." I gasped. That sounded horrendous. Just hearing the words reminded me of a dark time in history when the bubonic plague killed thousands of people. Chills ran down my spine as I questioned, *Could I be seriously ill?*

"The doctor is a specialist and has helped many people with this illness. Try her. You've got nothing to lose."

Knowing instantly that John the mailman described my condition and was the messenger, I thanked my father in heaven for sending him to point the way. I scheduled the first of what became a series of appointments with the infectious disease doctor on the Upper East Side of Manhattan.

These visits were enlightening. Many women waited long hours in the waiting room for the doctor's help. We all had the same illness. Why was that? Was our culture pushing women far beyond their physical capabilities? Were women pushing themselves beyond their physical capabilities? Many of the patients were working women with children and simply trying to keep up with the pace of life. Something was wrong with this picture. Were these moms and working professionals putting too much pressure on themselves in the pursuit of happiness, empowerment, and fulfillment? I wondered how many were in crisis. Then it occurred to me: they all were. Our crises might be different; but just the same, we were all worn down.

The diagnosis was Epstein-Barr virus and chronic fatigue syndrome, for which there was no cure. The chronic bronchitis and poor digestive issues could be addressed. My body was completely run down, depleted of life-force energy, all brought on from being in crisis and not taking care of myself. The blood tests specific to my condition revealed certain aspects of my blood were abnormal. At least we now had something to address—major nutritional deficiencies and an incurable virus.

The doctor recommended a program of vitamin therapy including B-complex, potassium, magnesium, B12, and copper injections. Injections of B-complex could only be given in her office. She pushed the needle filled with a yellowish fluid into my vein, giving me a rush and natural high for a moment or two. The feeling was indeed grand! I learned how to inject myself with copper and B12. B12 was easy to administer. A quick fill of reddish liquid into the needle with a quick push into my arm actually became fun.

Copper injections were painful. Lidocaine, a local anesthetic mixed with liquid copper, eased the pain. I held my breath while inserting the needle into my thigh, hoping to avoid feeling the intense burning sensation as I ever so slowly pushed the handle downward to allow the clear mixture to seep under my skin. A painful black-and-blue lump always surfaced a few days afterwards.

Remembering the macrobiotic dietary changes my father incorporated into his diet when he first learned he had cancer, I gave it a try. Eating certain macrobiotic foods—such as brown rice, seaweed, and tofu—was supposed to help build a weakened immune system, but some foods were simply unpalatable.

Learning to take care of and respect my body was the lesson because the price I paid for being negligent was enormous. Continuing with this routine for a few months, my body improved slightly, but it was not enough. Something more was needed, something unknown, something yet to be revealed.

My second husband and I remained friends after the divorce and occasionally had dinner together. I often felt alone but was comforted by his concern for my health issues. He was always supportive. I kept praying our separation was a mistake and that we could go back in time and start over. Those prayers weren't answered; nor was the picture of the future clear.

My relationship with family and friends became distant as no one understood why my life was the way it was. Words such as "ungrateful" and "mixed-up," were spoken to me. And I was told I was an embarrassment. "You're divorced for a second time, Pauline. That's like living a Hollywood-style life." Perhaps I was mixed-up at the time, but I never felt embarrassed by the unfolding of my life. I stayed true to the course of my life, and if it meant that family judged the situation, then so be it. It is said that internal confusion is a high state of consciousness unfolding, as a person begins to break down old forms of conformity to find their true selves. An inner strength kept moving me forward, which I believe was the support of the Universe. Feeling tired, uncertain, and confused, I forged ahead into the unknown ... alone.

Conclusion: Looking back to reflect and heal is necessary to move forward in a new way. That which caused you to feel powerless is the very thing that will render you powerful. Don't ever give up on yourself. Your truest responsibility is to the Soul. Everything else is secondary.

CHAPTER 3

MIND-BODY, SOUL MATE, SYNASTRY

The human body is your temple and the physical matter in which the Soul's essence dwells in and around. Every organ, cell, bone, and tissue have their own minds and Soul energies to create wellness. The key is to bring mind, body, and Soul back into harmony, and health will be restored. When the obstacle of disease or dis-ease, as in disharmony in the body, is present, it represents a wake-up call from the Soul.

After a year of medical treatment, my physical condition improved slightly. It was early 1991, and my body still struggled to jump-start. I hoped the infectious disease doctor's treatment would be a miracle cure, but it was not. Before my father's death, my body was vibrant, full of life. Now I likened myself to a wilted flower, struggling to stand tall to reach the sun. A constant gray cloud seemed to hover over this wilted flower, yet momentary glimpses of hope peeked through the despondence. While those moments were rare, they were present. Maybe they were little messages from God to say, "Keep the faith, and don't ever give up." So I pushed onward in search of myself.

The Round Table

I continuously thanked God for my job. As assistant property manager-liaison of an elite midtown office building, my position offered a purpose of sorts. Upscale tenants in the building kept me on my toes, making me earn every penny of my generous salary. The purpose of a liaison for the landlord was to keep everyone happy. Oddly, while striving to accomplish this, my own life was in disarray, unclear, and out of control.

I adopted a daily motto culled from the song "Crazy He Calls Me" by Linda Ronstadt. To paraphrase, I'll do the difficult now; the impossible may take a little longer. With that mindset I managed a variety of colorful characters, from a maniacal landlord to overentitled tenants.

An urgent meeting was scheduled at the last minute, and all managers were required to attend. Dressed in my navy-blue suit, I scurried to get to the big round table by 9:00 a.m. Tired from lack of sleep in those days, I generally found early morning meetings stressful. The combination of a 6:00 a.m. wake-up and praying the subway connections would be on time caused more fatigue. One morning I fainted on the subway train while in motion and awoke to find myself on the grimy floor. Numerous eyes starred at me; no one extended a hand to help. "Oh, excuse me. I must have fallen," I blurted out, pulling myself up off the filthy floor, not remembering where I was for a moment. "I'm sorry. Did I fall on top of you?" I asked a few people sitting in front of me. They shook their heads as if immune to what had just happened. Standing with weakened legs, sweat ran down my face and body, drenching my clothes. I wondered, *Will I ever be healthy again?* My purse, however, remain clutched around my arms. For this I was grateful.

That day I was on time. It was a serious meeting. Every important person in the organization attended, including two new faces. The chief of operations, Mr. M., often noted for his capricious decisions, had fired the elevator contractor who until then had been servicing ninety-eight elevators in nine buildings. The meeting's agenda was to introduce Steve and Lou, two well-known elevator guys who would be responsible for implementing a plan to assure perfect functioning of the elevators. *Good luck to them*, I thought.

Steve was a sophisticated negotiator who seemed to be an advocate for women in business. But it was Lou who got the attention of the women in the room. Tall and well-built, with a chiseled face and salt-and-pepper hair, he attracted all of us. His brown eyes, soft voice, yet masculine aura set off an inner giggle for single and married women alike.

After the meeting, the women's restroom was abuzz with gossip about the new contractors. "How do we complain to such attractive guys?" asked a colleague. "The same way you do an unattractive one," I replied, refreshing my sallow complexion with another coat of rose frost lipstick.

Basically, elevator contractors worked for building management. Every assistant manager in charge of daily operations was a woman. We were given permission to complain and do whatever was necessary to keep all elevators functioning to accommodate our elite clientele. I was fortunate to work for a progressive company whose policies provided equal opportunities for women, which was rare in those days. Striving for perfection, I used my power and position to get what was needed; I complained incessantly!

After six months or so of dealing with my wrath, Lou invited me for a drink. Surely his motives were to calm the obsessive complaints that came from my office. This guy was unaware that I was ill, spiritually empty, and downright exhausted. My ability to negotiate or be reasonable was impaired by the run-down condition of mind and body. My Soul was nowhere in sight.

It was late November 1991 when we walked into the Water's

Edge restaurant overlooking the East River and sat at the sprawling wood bar. Festive Christmas decorations brought a cheery feeling to the ambiance to its old-world décor. Scalloped draped curtains, sewn of burgundy velvet and gold tassels, hung from a vast array of windows, offered enchanting views of New York City's sparkling wonderland.

"Two glasses of Cabernet coming right up," confirmed the distinguished-looking gentleman tending bar.

I was waiting for a diplomatic plea from Lou to slow down the persistent flow of complaints coming from my office. Instead he talked about his younger years, when he left New York on a whim to explore the Dakotas. He openly talked about traveling into the rugged Northwest Territory to explore Alaska to become a wild salmon fisherman.

"We had to kill a bear. It got into our food pantry, and once a bear gets into your food pantry, it never leaves."

"You killed a bear!" I gasped.

"I didn't, but my partner and a local Alaskan did. When you're living in the wilderness, sometimes it has to be done. It's either the animal or you."

I thought, *I'm having a drink with a modern day Jeremiah Johnson!* I was completely charmed.

Apparently elevator talk was not on the agenda. Subsequently, I stopped complaining about the elevators.

Soul Mates

Slowly, Lou and I began to get together as friends. He was labeled the eternal bachelor, which was attractive to me, someone in limbo, seeking aloneness to find herself. But at the end of one of our nice friendship dates, Lou sweetly expressed how much he enjoyed our friendship. I agreed it was a nice friendship. Never expecting him to want more than our occasional dinner and conversation, he said, "I enjoy your company. I'd like to expand our relationship to the next level, if that's okay with you."

"Expand?" I asked, almost choking on the word. The word "expand" was symbolic of our forthcoming life together, and on some level I knew it. Our karmic Soul agreement kicked in. "I'd like that very much."

Soul Mates show up when they are needed to assist in some area of your life and theirs. The highest purpose of all relationships is for internal growth. Soul Mate relationships are based on unconditional love at the Soul level. This relationship supports and challenges each partner to become better versions of themselves on the human level while being the perfect mirror to our dark sides and our light sides. This special person can be of the same or opposite gender, and will lift you up in dark times, and conversely, pull you down if you get too full of yourself. These relationships may or may not be romantic.

We cannot predict how long these relationships will last. It all depends on whether or not both partners continue to grow together. Having a true Soul Mate is not only about loving each other; it's about learning to love the self. It's impossible for one person to be *your* everything. When we learn to love ourselves, the outer world generously reflects that back to us in all areas of our lives.

We said good night, and as I approached the front door of my apartment, rummaging through my purse for keys, a weird thought came over me: *I'm going to marry this man.* I feared repeating past patterns and wasn't ready to be committed. Gently banging my head against the entrance door, whispering under my breath I spoke, "God, please, not again!" God did not listen. There's no escaping something that is destined. From that moment, Lou and I were united.

A Message from Heaven

With my earnings and a small inheritance from my father, I could afford to travel and buy whatever I needed. Truthfully, I hated the inheritance. I'd have given back every dollar of it to have my father alive. But for the degree of financial security it provided, I was deeply grateful.

Then in June 1992, the unthinkable happened. The financial security I enjoyed was threatened by a layoff of many employees in upper-management positions. A lagging economy gave corporate offices the perfect excuse to lay off higher-paid employees. I was one of them. After devoting eight years of my life to this company, renewing leases and maintaining excellent tenant relations, I was awarded a pink slip for my services. I was hurt, angry, embarrassed, and in ten days, unemployed.

But sometimes what appears to be the worst situations are blessings in disguise. The Universe has a plan.

After several interviews for which I was completely qualified, not one job offer came through. I stopped the job search and took the summer off. The thought of an absent 6:00 a.m. ringing alarm clock was welcomed. Maybe some much-needed rest would cure me. With lots of time to do nothing, my mind was consumed with thoughts about myself, my life, and my father.

It seems that when we lose a loved one, the loss can open the door for us to begin to understand that life after death continues. The longing to reconnect with them sparks our curiosity to explore the afterlife. This innate yearning is strong because it is the Soul's way of getting our attention.

It was a Monday evening when I decided to stay in my apartment alone. Thoughts about the future kept bombarding my mind. *Where am I going? What am I going to do once the summer is over?* The moderate severance pay I received wouldn't last forever. Just before going to bed, I asked my father for guidance. "Daddy, if you can hear me, please help me. I don't know where my life is headed and need your advice. What should I do next? Where should I go? What's going to happen?" After speaking those words aloud into the air, into nothingness, I felt sleepy. For the first time in three years, the sandman showered me with fairy dust. Drifting off into a deep sleep, I was given the greatest gift of my life. I was allowed to visit my father in heaven.

I'm traveling through some kind of portal into outer space. It's very light and bright in here. My body feels buoyant, not heavy, tired, or sick. The feeling is total freedom as I fly upward into the night sky. As much as I try to control where I'm going, I can't. An unknown presence is in control, but I feel safe. Suddenly, I see my father. He's standing in front of me and looks exactly the way he did while alive and healthy. His big smile is radiant, just the way I remember him. I'm overwhelmed with feelings of love by our reunion. Behind him is a vibrant bright white light with soft shades of pink and blue. The white light is too bright to look directly into; it hurts my eyes. The image of my father is clear. His new life seems to suit him well.

My heart races with excitement. I reach out to touch him, but some kind of barrier prevents me from doing so. His spirit lives in the heavenly realm while my spirit is still living in the earthly realm; for this reason we are not permitted to touch. The love and peace are wonderfully irresistible here. For what seems like only a few moments, I bask in this loving grace. Although I try to speak with words, it is impossible. Verbal communication is nonexistent when in spirit. What remains is telepathic communication by way of thought and feeling.

He looks directly into my eyes. His mouth does not move, yet I hear his voice. He speaks in the form of thoughts, Go back to school. Go back to school. Go back to school. Call Franklin College, get transcripts, go back to school. Get your degree.

The dream shifts to show images of when I attended this college in 1977. Picturesque images of Switzerland, the mountains, and green valleys are brought forth from a happy memory bank. Then, all the images disappear and go blank.

Waking from that unusually peaceful sleep, I recollected the dream and my father's message. It was clearly and profoundly embedded in my memory. The morning sun shone brightly through my bedroom window, turning the light gray walls into the same pale-blue hue seen shining behind my father in heaven. Surely it was a sign. A knowing of truth was concretely implanted into my mind. The first step was revealed. I jumped out of bed with sleepy eyes, blurry from a generous supply of fairy dust. Still in pajamas, I dialed the international operator to connect to Franklin College in Lugano, Switzerland. Transcripts were now on the way to Forest Hills, New York. Studying for eighteen months left me one semester shy of earning an associate's degree.

The energy of the dream lingered for a few weeks. During this time, I was aware that traveling into heaven resulted in some kind of healing and upgrade in my health for which I was grateful. The dream was clairvoyant and provided authentic guidance from a deceased relative that felt as real as you reading this book right now.

My mind was unusually clear and decisive for about three to four weeks after heaven's visit. Answers to questions came immediately upon asking. Which school was I to return to? Which course of study was now appropriate? Within one week the right college presented itself, St. John's University, with just the perfect curriculum in human resource management. In January 1993 I was headed back to college at age thirty-four to obtain a bachelor's degree. My goal was to be a human resource director for a large corporation.

While I was intimidated by the thought of going back to school, the challenge awakened a new kind of inner power, following my inner truth regardless of what others were doing in their lives. While friends were married and raising children, I was in search of myself and the meaning of life. My life *was* different. A new feeling emerged: acceptance. I began to accept how uniquely my life was unfolding despite how different it looked as compared to others. Slowly I learned it's okay to be different, it's okay to follow the road less understood, it's okay to be *me* despite the deep insecurities about it.

Only one little glitch remained in the process. If I were to return to school, how would I continue to support myself financially, including paying for tuition? My financial resources were limited and would not sustain my independence for the next three years. I wondered, *Will I have to move back home with my mother for a few years?* As torturous as this would be for me and her, I would sacrifice myself now for my future. I told Lou about the dream and my desire to return to college.

Two weeks later, I woke up in Lou's apartment to the scent of coffee percolating. He was preparing our Sunday morning breakfast ritual with mixed fruit, coffee, and toasted Irish scones with butter. I dragged my body out of bed and walked into the kitchen. I turned on the stereo to our favorite country music station. The song "Colors of the Wind" always touched our hearts as it played softy in the background. The specific lyrics of a wolf's cry to the blue corn moon ran chills down my spine each time I heard the song. Something about the wilderness of nature and a full moon stirred inexplicable desires to be free and passionate.

"Let's have breakfast on the balcony." He pointed to the two chairs on the terrace of the sixth-floor apartment. It was August, and the sun shone through the glass doors into the living room, radiating warmth.

"Oh, how nice," I said. "You've prepared breakfast." I felt safe and cared for. Smiling, I grabbed my cup of coffee and a scone as I slid toward the balcony and sat in the sun-warmed chair.

"I've been thinking about your dream and have an idea, if you are open to it." I listened intently. "Why don't we move in together? I'd release this apartment lease and move in with you. This way you will be close to the university, making travel easy. And actually, your apartment location is easier for me to travel into the city."

I couldn't believe my overjoyed ears! "I don't have any income now, and school will be a priority," I replied.

"I will handle the bills. You figure out how to pay for tuition. I think this is a good move for both of us. We can make preparations to move in January or February."

Without hesitation, I welcomed the invitation. We were falling in love, and the timing was perfect. I leaned over to kiss him on the cheek. His hand held mine as we began to plan our future.

Medicine from the Earth

Being health conscious was becoming more important. I often shopped at local Korean grocers who offered a variety of organic fresh fruits and vegetables. Back then the word "organic" was a foreign concept to many people. It makes enormous sense to ingest naturally grown food. Why did we ever start adding chemicals to our food supply or create food from chemicals?

Going to a local health food store became a weekend priority, and it was like walking into a new world. Unfamiliar foods filled the shelves awaiting exploration. I was excited by the new food selection. There's no doubt a higher vibration emanated from organic foods. Pamphlets on detoxification programs caught my interest. Detoxing and fasting are not easy for us Westerners. Starting slowly with a one-day detox, eating only fruits and vegetables, then gradually growing comfortable with two days, then three is very beneficial to building a strong immune system. Years later we were able to easily fast for three days, which resulted in a clear mind and energized body.

One visit to the local health food store awakened a past-life passion of mine. "Take a look at this," Lou said, handing me a booklet with herbal remedies formulated by Linda Rector Paige.

Quickly flipping through the book, I saw herbal formulas for chronic fatigue, adrenal fatigue, and other infections. Natural herbal formulas synergistically composed to heal various conditions. Somehow I knew these beautiful herbs would help!

I walked over to the section where several shelves were lined with herbal tinctures. Excitement stirred through my body just eyeing the bottles with names I could not yet pronounce. One by one, I filled the shopping basket with many tinctures recommended in the booklet. An innate knowing, a familiarity, a déjà vu moment flashed through my mind. Had I worked with natural medicine in a past life? I later learned this to be true. A hidden passion remained dormant until many magical herbal tinctures lined up on the shelf sparked an innate knowing from the distant past.

Years later I learned from a past-life regressionist that indeed, herbal medicine was a passion of my Soul. Centuries ago I was the daughter of an alchemist. My passion was to work with him in the laboratory. But as I grew up, I was forced to marry and have children against my wishes. In those days, it was considered improper for a woman not to marry. Following social law, I left my father and the laboratory I loved to live a life acceptable to society. Learning this about my past life enriched my understanding of who I was and the life I was currently living.

On returning home from the health food store, I began experimenting with mixing formulas in hopes of healing myself. A Soul desire to study herbal medicine emerged as it felt right and brought feelings of joy, passion, and purpose. The beginning of my Soul purpose was being revealed and carried out in this lifetime.

I do not believe we can figure out our Souls' purpose. Only through an awakening and connection with something intangible, such as deep desire and sparking interest when it shows up, is what leads us toward life purpose. When we connect with the desire of the Soul, not the mind, we will be internally guided through intuition on what to do. Life purpose is a constant unfolding of personal evolution.

Fascinated by herbs and their medicinal potential, I studied them with gusto. Without reservation, I began to concoct my own herbal formulas to address specific symptoms. Apparently I drew upon past-life wisdom. The alchemist within had been awakened.

Within one week of taking many tinctures, my body felt a bit stronger. One formula cleansed the liver; the other strengthened the kidneys and adrenal glands. Yet, another was to fight infection. Chronic fatigue and the Epstein-Barr virus are combinations of adrenal fatigue, an overgrowth of yeast and bacteria, immune deficiency, and emotional stress. Finally, I was taking care of my body with wholesome food and herbal medicine.

Herbs became my life, my cure-all, and my love. Instead of a medicine cabinet full of pharmaceuticals, a kitchen cabinet was devoted to herbal tinctures of all kinds. Herbs are pure love. They are God-given. Every food and herb that grows from our beloved Earth is meant to heal us in some way. Not to mention the body is familiar with herbal medicine on an ancient cellular level, thereby making herbs an excellent choice for healing and rebuilding the body. Herbs are considered concentrated foods of very high vibration. They are your body's dream to heal, nourish, and rebuild itself.

Shortly thereafter, friends and family consulted with me on which herbs could heal their ailments. Somehow I knew exactly which ones to recommend. My reputation as an herbal healer spread. Years later I studied formally through the School of Natural Healing and became a master herbalist.

> For every human illness, somewhere in the
> world there exists a plant which is the cure. There is
> a healthy potential locked inside these plants which

is integral with their evolution, just as it is part of human evolution to learn to tap this wonderful gift of nature. (Rudolf Steiner)

Breath Medicine

Throughout my life I used aerobic exercise and weight lifting to keep in shape. But I was still too weak and tired for those exertions. Then an unusual thing happened. The word "yoga" burst into my mind. *Yoga?* I thought. *Why yoga? Daddy, are you telling me to try yoga?*

I remembered an assignment given to me by my sixth-grade teacher to write a ten-page book report on India. I envisioned the photos of yogis, with their legs and arms twisted around their bodies as they meditated for days in this position without food. In the early 1990s, Western culture was unfamiliar with yoga, and so was I. *Oh goodness, I'll never be able to do that! Am I supposed to become a yogi?* I prayed not.

Then, as God would have it, an infomercial with Jane Fonda practicing yoga appeared on TV. How fortuitous! I began to make a connection between my thoughts and the manifestation of them. It seemed that whatever I needed miraculously showed up. Without hesitation, I ordered the video to learn yoga from the actress.

Yoga was different and new. Learning how to breathe properly and gently move my body into postures that heal, release, and calm was an entirely new concept from pumping iron and intense cardio classes. At first I was awkward when practicing the postures. I felt like an inflexible iron rod trying to soften, bend, and twist into unfamiliar positions. Sometimes I felt frustrated. My mind and body were not yet connected. As I watched Jane Fonda instruct with fluidity and grace, slowly my body succumbed to the movements with ease. The new exercise was breath medicine to open the lungs, heart, and life-force energy. Learning how to move that breath down into my belly and organs slowly helped revive a once-exhausted body. Again my health improved, but it was not enough. Some degree of fatigue and insomnia remained constant. The search continued.

The Revelation

One night Lou and I went to see the movie *My Life*. In this film, Michael Keaton plays a husband who has cancer, and his wife seeks every possible treatment for his recovery. She explores traditional medicine but also explores alternative healing methods. As we watched the movie, one scene in particular caught my attention. The husband is lying on a table, and the Chinese healer places his hands about six inches above his body. The healer psychically sees parts of the husband's life that have contributed to the cancer and tells him that he must release anger from the past and forgive his father because that is at the root of the disease. The husband denies his anger at first. Then he admits it but refuses to forgive the past. Michael's character fails to acknowledge the message of his disease and dies in the end.

Watching that movie scene roused my first revelation. "That's it!" I exclaimed. The unorthodox treatment was what I needed to heal my diseases. I just knew it. I wondered where would we find such an unconventional, shaman-type person.

"What do you mean?" Lou asked.

"That treatment, the hands thing, what the Chinese man was doing. That's what I need to heal my illnesses."

Lou looked at me in the strangest way.

"Where would we find such a person?" I pressed.

"I don't know, but we'll go to China or Japan if we need to."

My love exploded for him in that moment. His tone was serious, expressing genuine concern. My heart opened, feeling vulnerable and overjoyed with love. I hadn't felt that way since before my father died. I felt protected and cared for by this gentle yet strong man. I wondered why he wanted to be with me, a sickly person with a pale complexion, who was always tired, and much too skinny. Yet, Soul Mate relationships are meant to support each other for the sake of healing, love, growth, evolution, and to complete karmic contracts— which are agreements between Souls before human incarnation. Ours was underway. He became my rock.

We did not know what this healing method was but had to find it. We called it "moving hands around the body to cure illness." The search for a healer began. I never imagined the life-changing events that would happen next. God was surely in control.

Behind every disease is a message from your Soul. If you have been diagnosed with disease—or pain, cancer, diabetes, acne, or any other condition—the question that must be asked is, "Why have I created this disease?" You created the disease. Therefore, you have the power to undo and reverse disease through an exploration of why it was created and what message the imbalance is trying to impart.

Disease is usually based in a disconnection to yourself and God. Emotions and thoughts are the first causes of all dis-ease. Although you cannot see the emotional or mental bodies, you can feel them, and they are very real. To heal disease or disharmony in the physical body, we must return to the first cause of the problem, the circumstances, emotions and thoughts that caused it.

Suppressed emotions and negative thoughts create blockages and imbalances in the emotional and mental energy bodies, resulting in a physical condition we call disease. Where are they suppressed? Look at where your disease has manifested, and you will find the suppressed emotions or thoughts. Most times emotions and thoughts are suppressed with good intention as a way to cope with situations that are deeply hurtful. In turn, the intellect takes over and says, "Suppress the emotions and thoughts that hurt, and you won't feel it." Suppression is not healing, it is avoiding and denying that which needs to be addressed. By avoiding life's lessons, feelings, emotions, and thoughts, dis-ease is created subconsciously and will keep you from moving forward in a healthy way. Heal the emotional and mental bodies, and the cells of the physical body will naturally respond toward good health.

Hereditary or ancestral patterns are another cause of disease. Passed down from generations these patterns are rooted in our subconscious. When a hereditary pattern is diagnosed, such as heart disease, cancer or any other medical condition, is your first thought negative? Is your first feeling fear? Or do you have the deep trust in your inner healing ability to overcome the condition and restore all aspects of your health? Believe you have the power to heal yourself with the help of doctors and natural healers.

Take care of your physical body by eating healthy foods. Junk foods are low-vibration foods. Notice when a challenging situation occurs, the first foods we tend to gravitate toward are sugar, fats, and alcohol. Low-vibration foods contribute to lowered mental acuity and immunity, preventing the body's natural defense system to work properly.

Another cause of disease is we became too attached to the physical reality and are living too much from an outer perspective rather than an inner perspective. This is an opportunity to evolve into higher states of consciousness. Deeper issues here can be the need for self-love, self-worth, forgiveness and compassion, empathy, or self-empowerment.

A simple exploration exercise to uncover the message of your disease is to look at what was happening in your life around the time the disease started. Often there are many clues to be explored during this period of your life. Sometimes the disease shows up years or even lifetimes after the initial issue was first experienced. When this happens, a deeper and longer investigation is required. Layer upon layer of suppressed issues must be uncovered and released little by little.

The mind must be trained to accept new ways of thinking. Thoughts can be limited or expansive, positive or negative. We must pay attention to our thoughts, emotions, feelings, traumas, and challenging situations. Our bodies speak the language of all our life experiences, which are not mistakes but by divine design meant to wake us up, explore ourselves, and evolve.

Since the body is subservient to the thought patterns of the mind, it makes sense to think positively and correct a negative mind. Thank your body for its innate ability to function. Thank your liver for detoxifying the blood. Thank your stomach for digesting foods, and the small intestine for absorbing nutrients. Thank your bones and muscles for giving you physical strength to walk, exercise, and move. Thank your heart for circulating oxygenated blood to your body, and your lungs for their capacity to allow you to breathe. Thank your adrenal glands for producing ATP, the hormone that gives you energy. Thank your eyes which give you the sight to see beauty, and ears which allow you to hear loving words. Recognizing the body's natural ability to function is a wonderful way to connect with your physical body. As you connect with your body and organs, don't be surprised if they start taking to you through intuitive messages. Usually, these messages will alert you to the foods they want, and don't want. Simply pay attention to the urges. You have the power to reverse a disease and heal completely. Your body has been innately programmed for perfect health. A clean, healthy body allows the Soul to speak and thrive through an uncluttered mind.

Conclusion: Everything you seek is seeking you. The greatest investment you'll ever make to create an abundant life is in yourself. The future we desire cannot be created until we evolve the present moment. The evolution of now is our pathway to a glorious future.

Chapter 4

The Baggage Handler

In December 1993 Lou and I attended a black-tie affair for juvenile diabetes. It was a cold day in Manhattan, yet somehow the glistening lights of this magical city stirred up feelings of excitement and being alive. We often attended these fundraising galas, but this night felt different.

I walked over to our table and found an empty seat. Lou sat down next to me. Feeling a bit foggy and tired, I hoped this group wouldn't find me rude if I remained on the quiet side rather than engaging in conversation. It took too much energy to think and talk. The beautiful black-velvet dress I wore hung loosely around my underweight body.

A woman sat next to Lou. She was the wife of one of his guests. They struck up a conversation. Cautiously, she mentioned what she did for a living. Lou turned to me with eyes wide open and said, "You need to switch seats with me and talk to this lady."

"Why?" I questioned, feeling upset that I might need to converse with someone.

"Just switch," he insisted. "I think she's a moving hands person!"

"Really? Seriously? How can that be?" I asked. But he was adamant, so I shifted over to his chair and smiled at the woman now sitting next to me. We exchanged a few pleasantries about the event, and engaged in small talk for a few minutes, then I asked, "What do you do?"

"I work with energy. I'm a healer." Her voice was gentle. "I don't usually discuss my work because most people don't understand, but I sense you do."

Initially I felt cautious to speak with her yet excited by the possibility that such a person actually existed right here in New York City. Was she real? Could this be fate?

"I think I do, and I've been looking for someone to help me. I saw a movie recently with a Chinese man moving his hands over a person's body to heal him of cancer. You know, like a moving hands around the body to heal type person. I think I need something like this to help me."

The woman did not make eye contact with me. It seemed she was ignoring my words as she gazed out into space. I continued to explain my physical condition, how doctors couldn't find anything seriously wrong with me except low nutritional counts, which were being addressed, and how tired and sickly I was since being diagnosed with chronic fatigue syndrome. She didn't acknowledge the explanation of my condition, then she asked, "May I run my hands a few inches over your body?"

Filled with intrigue I said, "Please do."

The healer moved her hand up and down my midsection under our table. Somehow I felt heat radiate from her hand. Initially I doubted what she was doing, but then I felt flabbergasted by how real this was. People were talking and dancing, and no one noticed what we were doing.

Every now and then Lou peeked over to see what was happening. "Everything going okay over here?"

I nodded, but I couldn't speak. It was extraordinary and exciting. Her hands were about six inches above my body. She was doing exactly what the Chinese man in the movie did!

"Your body is only functioning at about fifty percent of your energy capacity," she firmly stated.

"That doesn't sound very good," I responded. "It makes sense given the fatigue and chronic conditions. Can you help? I'm desperate!" I kept rambling on, trying to fill in the conversation with more information about my condition, hoping she would provide more insights.

"So you're a moving hands around the body to heal person?" I asked.

She handed me her business card, "Call me on Monday. We will set an appointment for you. Yes, I'm a moving hands around the body to heal person." She smiled.

"The correct name is simply, energy healer." She was lovely. I liked her proper English mannerisms.

If her energy diagnosis was correct, it would certainly explain why I continued to experience fatigue even after all the treatments from the infectious disease doctor, yoga, dietary changes, and my herbal remedies. An appointment was set with her for the following week. Luckily, she lived twenty minutes from my apartment. Travel to Asia wasn't necessary after all.

It was rare to find this type of person in those days. God brought her to me in a way I never could have imagined. When we ask the Universe for something we need, we must be open to how and when it will arrive. We cannot orchestrate these occurrences; we must simply follow the inner guidance.

Healing Begins

My first session with the energy healer was profound. I walked into her healing room and saw a massage table and many shelves filled with vitamin supplements. The walls were pastel-pink, and one was covered with a beautiful hand-painted mural of a vine with green leaves and flowers. The energy in the room felt calm and exuded a feeling that all was well, despite the jittery anticipation in my stomach.

The healer was thin and probably middle-aged. Her short, light-brown hair was parted on the side, sweeping over her forehead. She wore a plain white T-shirt with a pair of khaki chinos. Her strong English accent made it difficult to understand all her words, but the sound of her voice was still soothing.

"Lie down and make yourself comfortable," she softly instructed.

I followed her instructions anxiously, like a good patient, and made myself as comfortable as I could, given my anxiety level. She began tapping on my wrist. She explained that she was communicating with my body and receiving information from me through kinesiology.

How is she communicating with my body? I wondered. *Is this real? Maybe it's all a bunch of nonsense.* I thought it was like something out of a sci-fi movie, but it sure seemed real. She was confident using her own system of kinesiology, a method to communicate with the body using muscle-testing response. Apparently she was asking my body questions and receiving answers.

The room was quiet for a minute or so. My eyes were glued to her as I watched closely, trying to make logical sense of what was happening. Of course there is no logic in this process. You either believe or you don't. I believed in the metaphysical world. It was happening! She continued to tap my wrist and then wrote words and phrases on a sheet of unlined white paper, mumbling under her breath. I couldn't tell if she was talking to me or herself.

"Excuse me, are you speaking to me?" I asked. Shaking her

head back and forth, she continued to work. Curiosity was killing me, so I turned to look at what she was writing and asked, "What are you writing?" She ignored my question. I got the impression she was slightly annoyed by my curiosity.

A few moments later she looked at me with her soft brown eyes and said, "Are your parents alive?" Hearing this, I began to choke up and used every ounce of my energy to keep from crying.

"My mother is alive. My father died about five years ago." My voice quivered. A tear slid down the right side of my face, and I felt embarrassed by my emotions. Putting her hand gently on my shoulder, her eyes filled with compassion.

"I'm so sorry for your loss," she said. "Please let yourself cry. You are holding in so much grief it's killing you."

An uncontrollable flow of tears welled up in my eyes. I couldn't stop it and felt powerless and ashamed of myself. Something came over me, and I could not control my physical reaction. I felt so vulnerable and embarrassed by my inability to control my emotions. Lying on my back, water poured out of my eyes, forming a pool inside my ears. My nose dripped with mucous, and I had difficulty breathing. She handed me a pile of tissues.

"It's okay. Let yourself grieve."

"It's okay?" Those words sounded foreign. When my emotions surfaced as a child, I learned how to be an expert suppressor of them as a matter of survival. A flash of my childhood rearing reminded me that I was taught to hold in my feelings and not let myself look stupid or vulnerable by expressing them. Hearing her words gave me permission to cry, to let go and to feel. I started to relax. For the first time ever, my feelings were being acknowledged, and it was acceptable to express them. But silently I still questioned, *Is it really okay to cry and express my emotions to others?*

I cried throughout the entire healing session as the recollection of my father's death returned vividly to my mind. Although I had cried many times for the loss of my dad, the energy of that loss was still present. Obviously she knew the grief of his passing was part of the foundation of my illness.

In a subsequent healing session, the issue of my first marriage surfaced. Again I cried throughout the session. Although I thought I had worked through the issues of my first divorce in the office of tears and meeting with him, the healing sessions revealed that the energy of hurt and disappointment lingered deeply in the subconscious of my pain body.

Soon I learned that we have numerous energy bodies, including intuitional, mental, emotional, etheric, physical, and pain. These energy bodies are explained in Chapter 8.

Her hands were placed over my body and then over my head. She moved around the room, standing in one corner and then another corner. She asked me to repeat words and phrases, some of which made logical sense; some did not. So many unusual yet wonderful things occurred during these sessions. After a few months of treatment I began to feel lighter. The healer often explained how the layers of life's challenges need to be peeled back like the layers of an onion. This is how we release the past and open to a new, healthy mind and body. The smile that had faded away because of life's hardships slowly returned. New beginnings were now possible as the layers of life's hardship released.

Oddly, grieving with awareness enables us to heal on many levels we aren't conscious of. Be aware of what you are grieving. Is it anger? Hurt? Betrayal? Disappointment? Insecurity? Allowing the tears of grief to flow in a visceral way is a powerful way to heal. Letting tears flow like a baby's cry will release emotions connected to the present, as well as timelines and experiences from long ago. Tears are connected to our emotions which directly affect the wellness of the physical body. Releasing shame of feeling your emotions will allow the river of tears to flow, and as this happens, something amazing occurs. Emotions of the present, past, subconscious past, and past life connect to current grief, and they are released forever. It's as if every emotion that has been locked up for ages is now magnetized to the current stream of tears, finally being released from deep within your memory bank. And behind those tears is the power of your Soul, waiting to be acknowledged.

We're never too old to cry. There is beauty in allowing grief to heal you. Processing grief in this way can take time to develop, as our natural reaction is to shut down, which can cause depression, anxiety, or disease.

Past Lives Play a Role

Some healing sessions went back into prior lifetimes. One experience I recalled was extremely powerful. It took place several centuries ago. I was a male about twenty-one years of age. I was pushed by another person into an abyss, where I drowned. During the healing session, I felt calm as I floated into peaceful realms. The energy healing always brought a feeling of peace, balance, and uplift. In her mind's eye, the healer witnessed the past event unfolding in scenes as she uttered words to describe my death. "Falling, crashing, gasping, asphyxiation, death." The words felt meaningless to me at the time. Leaving her home I felt physically well, with feelings of joy.

As a child, I had many recurring dreams. I'd dream each dream three times, then they would be permanently gone, never to be dreamed again. Even as a child, I was aware that there was something about the number three or experiencing something three times that created healing on a deeper level I was not yet in tuned with. Three is a divine number.

The past life healing session reminded me of one recurring dream. I recalled feeling sensations of falling from a high place, while the pit of my stomach felt like it was dropping in fear. Then, I was underwater trying to breathe. In the dream-state I seemed to have the ability to reconstruct the scene so that somehow I was able to breathe underwater. My mind would say, *Just breathe Pauline. This is a dream and you can control it.* I seemed to have some kind of magical power to be able to do this. In my life, I never feared the ocean or a river. I did fear drowning or not being able to breathe. Many years later the recurring dreams stopped.

A few days after the healing session, I began to experience headaches, nausea, coldness, sleeplessness, and most interestingly, the taste of salt water in my mouth. Each time I randomly burped, the taste of salt water was present. I'd wash my mouth out with fresh water and lemon. My head felt dizzy at times, and my eyesight intermittently blurry. Symptoms from this healing session lasted about two to three months and then finally subsided. The past-life event was fully purged from my etheric blueprint. Purging this past life changed something deep within, and afterwards I felt like a different person.

Throughout my life up to that point, I had always had a slight hearing problem. Hearing tests always indicated my hearing was perfect. But often when someone spoke, words sounded muffled. I couldn't hear exactly what they were saying and had to ask them to repeat their words. It seemed like a good idea to tell the healer this information. I called her regarding this insight.

"You've been persecuted in a past life," spoke the healer.

The twinge in my stomach indicated her words were true. "Was I ridiculed badly?" I began to feel nervous and nauseated.

"Have you seen the movie *The Scarlet Letter*?" she asked.

Pain in my stomach intensified, and my head began to spin. "Yes I have. I actually like that movie and how two lovers stayed true to their love despite what others thought or said about their affair."

"In your past lifetime you were persecuted several times, and you learned how to block out hurtful words of others. In my psychic vision I see you with your hands over your ears, trying to drown out the insults of the crowd," she explained.

Hearing this information, I connected the dots between the physical hearing symptom and the movie. I thanked her for the information. After we hung up, I sat on the living room couch and vowed to heal this on my own. I didn't know how to heal myself, but the intention to do so kicked-in the innate healing power we all have.

At first I sat in silence for a while and then decided I'd try to go back into the past life myself. Closing my eyes, taking a few deep breaths, I spoke aloud to God and asked for help. Images began to show up. I was being screamed at by many people. For what, I wasn't sure. Nor did I need to know. Feelings of hurt and anger began to surface. A thought popped into my mind, *Who are these people to judge me?* The emotions were strong as I felt the words of others sting like daggers into my heart. I let myself cry and screamed aloud, "Stop! All of you stop! Stop screaming at me. Go home and look at yourself, and look at me no more!" These were the words I could not say back then, but I could say them now as part of my healing. Anger spewed through my words as I kept repeating them until I could speak no more. I rested for the balance of the day.

In the days after this purge my hearing became worse. Everything sounded muffled by static. Intuitively, I knew the hearing loss was temporary, so I decided to enjoy not hearing anyone speak for a few days, including myself. My ears felt like cotton balls were stuffed into them. Shortly thereafter, my hearing slowly returned.

It was this purge that led to the ability to become clairaudient not too long afterwards. Clairaudience is the ability to hear the words of spirit as clearly as hearing a person sitting next to you. One evening, I set my intention to be clairaudient, and instantly I was. When we are ready to experience the Soul's natural ability, the awakening happens automatically.

I realized that our Souls hold the memories of every experience from every lifetime in the etheric body blueprint. There are many ways to energetically heal the tragic events of human life, past or present through various types of energy work. Reiki, Somatic Therapy and Zero Balancing, are a few methods available. Another powerful modality is, viewing the Akashic Records (a vibrational library in the fifth dimensional reality, not an actual physical library), which contains all the information of the universe of all beings from the beginning of time and space. In the old and new testament of the bible it's called, The Book of Life. A skilled metaphysical practitioner can view these events in their mind's eye as a picture, or similar to a scene from a movie. Past life regression is another way to access traumatic events still operating causing repetitive problems, from long ago. Energy work heals on many levels, including the mental, emotional, physical, and spiritual. It can include past-life trauma, hereditary patterns, and karma.

Working with the healer was an extraordinary experience. According to her, my willingness to heal and let go of the past was something she had not encountered before. She explained that not everyone really wants to heal themselves because there's a secondary gain from remaining ill; attention and pity from others.

"You deeply desire to heal, and I promise you'll feel better fairly soon, Pauline." These were her spoken words to me quite often. I was unaware of my own willingness to heal, but hearing her say it brought comfort and reassurance. I trusted her. The grief from losing my father and from two divorces lifted from my heart, and my health slowly returned.

Once again the Universe provided me with exactly what was needed. I found herbal medicine and an energy healer to restore my health and well-being. Wanting to be healed, opening my mind, and learning to follow metaphysical signs put me on a different life path. It was all happening simultaneously. The Infinite Source was in control.

Years prior I surrendered, allowing God to lead the way forward, not knowing what I was getting myself into. It was all so perfectly designed by the Universe. It took a few years before my health was completely restored, but it was restored. For this I was deeply grateful.

All my energy bodies were releasing pent-up energy from the past. As a result, my physical body began to lighten up and heal from chronic illnesses. The human energy bodies play an enormous role in the ability to heal and awaken the Soul. When thoughts are too negative or emotions too strong, the physical body suffers as it carries the weight of suppressed energy.

Healing in this capacity really got me thinking about how every human experience we have has an effect on us physically, emotionally, mentally, and spiritually. Inquisitively, I began to observe just how much more healing was needed to free myself of the negative, burdensome experiences of many human lifetimes. Then I observed the world and everything and everyone in it and thought, *My goodness, we are on a long road back to Eden.*

Conclusion: Our wounds are not permanent unless we choose to ignore them. Heal and love yourself. You're worth it. Courageous is the Soul who looks deeper than the experience. What matters most is the awakening, not the experience itself.

Chapter 5

Intuition, Guides, Angels, Mediums, Fairies, and God

I can't imagine life without the guidance of spirit. Releasing the need to figure out the future opens the portal to be led by higher guidance, which always brings the outcome we really want. Intuition is a natural psychic ability that we all have. As part of your energy field, there exists a body of energy that I referred to earlier as the intuitional body. You have it whether you realize it or not, and it must be awakened and used as a tool to navigate through your life.

You've sensed the intuitive body when first meeting a person or walking into a room filled with strangers, and you get a vibe about a person or group of individuals. Spirits, angels, and God are around you all the time. They communicate with you through your intuition and openness. These nonphysical beings are here to help. It matters not who they are. What matters is that you acknowledge their existence and their willingness to help guide you. Human beings are not alone on the planet; we are assisted by many loving, enlightened energy beings.

Since sixteen years of age I believed in spirits, ghosts, angels, and God. The belief was not religious, it simply existed. I cannot give you a logical reason how or why I believed so strongly in metaphysical entities, I just did. No one talked about such things during my childhood. My parents did not believe in spirits, ghosts, or angels, but of course they believed in God as was taught by our religion.

My interest in psychic energy and spirits was ingrained in me and part of my programming. I remember the first time someone asked me if I believed in reincarnation. "Yes!" I exclaimed without thinking. To acknowledge these spiritual entities just seemed normal to me. Seeking the advice of psychics and engaging in séances started at an early age. As a child, I was energetically sensitive, but I did not realize just how sensitive I am until much later in life.

However, believing in spirit guides, angels, or God is not enough to fill the emptiness so natural to human beings. Nor is believing enough to make a solid connection with the spirit realm. Believing is the first step. The fact remains that it takes work and dedication to make the connection strong between two worlds. We must reach upward. It's not that the spirit world is so untouchable or far away. It's right here in front of us. The problem is human beings are naturally afraid of things they can't see or control.

Over the next several years, healing became a priority as my physical body returned to its natural healthy state. The intuitive body began developing on its own as my life healed. Impressions of psychic knowing resulted. I'd know who was calling when the phone rang, or information regarding myself or another would pop into my head. Intuition and connection to the spirit world began to change my life further. A strong desire to know more about who Pauline really was and why she was on this Earth was surfacing.

Spirit Guide

Regularly scheduled sessions with the healer not only healed my life and opened my intuitive nature, but my connection to the spirit world strengthened. A new nonphysical energy was present, and it did not feel like my father. Uncertain as to who or what this presence was or what it wanted, I was about to find out.

Lou and I were always challenged with communication issues. I talked too much, and he talked too little. One night we were experiencing one of our usual communication glitches. The conversation was not going well. At some point we abandoned the discussion and went to bed angry and frustrated.

It was the middle of the night, although I never looked at the clock. The room was dark. It felt like 2:00 a.m. or so, and something unusual happened.

I was sleeping soundly until my mind was disturbed by something mystical. I was abruptly awakened, but I was neither truly awake nor asleep. My body was sleeping, but my mind was alert. It seemed as though I entered a profound state of being between sleep and awake, the theta state. The theta state refers to the level of activity in the brain that occurs during sleep and dreaming.

> *My physical eyes are closed, yet I could see what is occurring before me through the inner-eye sight or psychic sight. A glowing white light enters the room through the window on my left. It starts out as a small ball of white light, floats into the center of the room, and stops at the edge of the bed. The light was too bright to look at directly. Curious and paralyzed, I could not take my mind's eye off it and observe it closely. At no point am I fearful. Instead, I am in awe of the mystical event unfolding right before my mind's eye. It is breathtakingly beautiful!*

The ball of light grows into a large sphere, and an image begins to appear in the center. At first I could not see it clearly. Then after a few moments, the face of an Asian woman appears, and I understand that her heritage is Japanese. Only the image of her head is visible, and she is strikingly beautiful. Black, silky, straight hair falls to her chin. The lovely, soft expression of her face indicates genuine care and concern. She is smiling while looking directly into my eyes. I focus on her lips as she speaks, "Give him time, give him time. Give yourself time, give yourself time." Instantly, I understand the message as it pertains to the way in which Lou and I communicate. Telepathically I ask, "How much time?"

The angel stares directly into my eyes. Her mouth is moving, speaking words, but I cannot hear them. I desperately try to glean every ounce of information being offered. It seems a switch had been turned off, and the volume is no longer audible. Something greater than the angel was in control of this supernatural visit. Then her image begins to fade out. Not wanting her to leave, I stare into her eyes, hoping to convey that I couldn't hear her final words and needed more information. The beautiful, loving face slowly disappears. I watch the white luminous light glide out of the window from which it came.

On waking the next morning, I clearly remembered the supernatural occurrence. Another magical experience was etched in my mind forever. It was real; it was lucid. I had been visited by an angel, and now I knew exactly who she was. Nothing was the same after that, and thank goodness change is constant.

I shared this experience with only the healer. Not many people believed in spirits, guides, or angel visits in those days. I expressed the experience to the healer on my next visit.

I lay on the healing table with a warm cotton blanket covering my body, and I felt safe. "Is it possible I could be visited by an angel during the night?" I curiously asked the healer.

"Well, yes of course, Pauline. What did it look like?" I explained the appearance of the image and how it floated in and out of the window.

"She is your current guide. She's not an angel. However, I do suggest you give her a name and call on her regularly."

"She's not an angel?" I felt confused.

"Angels do not appear as a human image with an ethnic heritage. They are pure spirit and often show themselves as light or even as an image of an angel with wings," she answered, smiling.

There is a difference. Guides have been in human form and have mastered human life. Angels have never been in human form, making them quite pure in nature. The job of the Japanese guide was to assist me to follow my path.

Finding just the right name became a slight obsession. I pondered giving her just the right one. The first impression I received was Angelica. Then I thought, *That is too corny, the angel, Angelica.* But she wasn't an angel; she was a guide.

One day while having my nails polished by my regular manicurist, who was named Delica, a light bulb went off in my head. The name Delica was beautiful and seemed like a good fit for the new Japanese guide. The name felt sort of right, and since I could not think of another one that I liked, Delica it was.

God Speaks

Shortly thereafter, another communication issue between Lou and me reared up. We got into a terrible argument, as so many couples do, over little silly things like being quiet when the other is sleeping or turning down the volume on the TV. It was just another of those instances when we simply could not agree. We were at an impasse. This lasted for several days, and my stomach and intestines churned with angst over the inability to resolve our problem. Pain developed in my stomach. Herbal formulas to heal were ineffective. I called the healer and described the symptoms. "You are Lou are in a power struggle," she said.

Every psychic, healer, and medium exemplified the ability to "know." It never ceased to amaze me how these people just knew what they knew. "Yes, we have been arguing without resolve." I acknowledged her accuracy.

"Meditate," she replied.

I thought, *Meditate? I don't know how to meditate.* "I've never meditated before in my life," I replied.

"Meditate at about five o'clock," she instructed.

How does one meditate when they don't know how? I winged it and figured if this is going to work, then it might not matter how I do it. Following her orders, I meditated at five o'clock. Not knowing what to do, I lay down on the bedroom floor. The plush gray carpet provided enough cushion as I lay on my back with palms facing upward, corpse pose in yogic terms, a small pillow placed under my head. I closed my eyes, took a few deep breaths, and began the prayer, "Our Father, who art in heaven, hallowed be thy name." I recall saying only a few verses of the prayer before I was swept away, taken upward into the Universe, where I conversed with God.

I traveled through a black portal, then it seemed I was in a large cosmos for a moment, and then the dialogue started. A conversation began in my mind, and I had no control over the voice of God or even my own voice in the form of thought, which I believe was my ego learning how to shift an old communication pattern. Every step of the dialogue was controlled by an essence much greater than I. The conversation happened automatically, yet I was part of it through observation.

Each time I was asked a question by God, I was given the opportunity to respond. Then I was instructed to ask the questions, and God replied. This energy force was extremely powerful, more so than with Delica. Specific instructions were given to me on how to communicate and how to resolve our conflict. I was being shown the way.

The Voice began to speak:

The Voice: What is wrong?

Me: My stomach hurts.

The Voice: Why does your stomach hurt?

Me: The conflict with Lou is upsetting me.

The Voice: What is the conflict about?

Me: Our inability to communicate.

Then the question-answer dialogue shifted. Now I was to ask the questions, and God gave the answers. Each time I asked a question, God answered with either a yes for correct or no for incorrect. Each time I received a no, I was given a chance to ask the question again to receive a yes. God was showing me how to communicate, but not by giving me the answers. Instead, I was being taught through my own mistakes and then shown how to correct them.

I asked God questions:

Me: Should I tell Lou he is at fault for our inability to communicate?

The Voice: No.

Me: Should I explain that most of our communication problems are his and that he needs to work on them?

The Voice: No.

Me: Should I tell him that he seems angry?

The Voice: No.

Me: Are some of the communication problems on my end?

The Voice: Yes.

Me: Should I say I feel hurt by our inability to communicate?

The Voice: Yes.

Me: Should I push him to respond?

The Voice: No.

Me: Should I wait for a response from him after I tell him how I feel?

The Voice: Yes.

Me: How long should I wait for a response?

God does not answer.

Me: Should I give him time, like a minute or longer to answer?

The Voice: Yes.

Me: Should I listen more?

The Voice: Yes.

The dialogue ended abruptly. I traveled back into my body and became aware of being back in the bedroom, on the floor. Exhausted from the experience, as I had never before held the energy of such a powerful being in my body, I rolled on to my left side and fell asleep and awoke about an hour later. I felt groggy on waking and reviewed the dialogue over and over until Lou arrived home at about seven o'clock.

The table was set with rose-colored dishes. A votive candle in the center of the table twinkled, and I smiled in hope God was with me. We sat down to dinner, and I used the new skills the Creator taught me. I opened the conversation by asking if he was willing to discuss some things that were happening. He agreed. I expressed how I felt in a most sincere way that was not accusatory. He was receptive but didn't answer directly. I pushed for an answer, which erased his willingness to communicate further. Using as much willpower as I could not to push further, I pushed anyway. Desperately wanting resolve, I couldn't summon the strength to give him the time he needed to respond. He became agitated, and then I backed down. We cleaned up the dishes, and he went into the living room to watch TV. The bedroom was my choice.

Later that night I reflected on how I had failed to follow God's teaching. Frustrated and disappointed by my failure, I sat on the bedroom floor, and asked for God's help again. No response was given. Had God abandoned me? I had hoped at the very least the spirit guide was still with me.

Suddenly an intuitive thought swept over me: *Don't beat yourself up, Pauline. Try, try again until you get it right. You've got a lot of work ahead of you. Tomorrow is another day.*

Releasing Blame

Spirit teaches us in a loving, nonjudgmental way. I learned to refine my own communication skills through this exercise. I was part of the problem. My partner and I were perfect mirrors for each other. Although I was the stronger communicator, my ability to speak from the heart was limited. Developing the ability to speak more gently would help the relationship. It seemed my job was to begin the healing of our communication patterns. Leading the way forward through example was key.

First principle of spirituality: Release the need to blame anyone, including yourself and God, for all the things that are less than perfect in life. Doing so will open the door for you to step into your true power. Blame is a dense emotion representing the act of punishment, and disempowerment, whether it be someone else or yourself. It is one of the most damaging emotional blockages to creating abundance. Personal healing releases the need to blame anyone, any situation or institution who has hurt, betrayed, misled, abused, or challenged you in any way. It is easy to blame others for how you feel about yourself or for the horrible things they did. The purpose of evolution and healing is to know your Soul, and embrace forgiveness through releasing blame. I'm not saying this is easy. Releasing blame takes inner work. Once the Soul begins to awaken, releasing blame becomes easier.

Moving forward, I learned to release blame of myself or another person as this mindset represented old paradigm thinking. Whenever I was triggered by someone or a situation, the answer was to look inward and transform myself. God taught me to speak about my feelings instead of projecting my feelings or putting words into the mouths of others, and to listen to their feelings as well. If we look at the world, we see how this dysfunctional pattern is prolific.

From this model, communication could go back and forth from person to person until a resolution was found, hopefully. This model provided real communication skills that involved speaking about how *you feel* instead of pointing a finger at what someone else did or didn't do.

The more responsibility you take for your life, the more power you will have to create a wonderful, abundant life. Moving beyond any need to finger-point will free your Soul and open your heart. Once you take responsibility to heal yourself and release the need to blame anything or anyone, the power you have over your life is profound. Take responsibility over the things you can control—you!

Remember, your Soul chose this life; it chose your parents and every challenging situation you were born into. Nothing is accidental. Your Soul knows you can overcome these difficulties. It is waiting for you to reconnect so you can co-create with God the life you have dreamed of living.

Who Me?

On days when healing sessions were scheduled, I was always filled with excitement, knowing something new would be revealed.

On one particular day, as the session came to an end, I lay on the table with eyes still closed, feeling peaceful, like I was floating on soft clouds, allowing the integration of new energy into my body.

"Pauline, do you know why you are here?" the healer asked.

I opened my eyes to see her standing at the foot of the table. "Oh yes. I'm here for you to heal me, and you have. I couldn't be well again without your help. I'm very grateful."

"There's something else for you to know. Our sessions haven't just been about you getting well. They are about you understanding why you are here." Her English accent was soft and low.

"Why I am here? What do you mean?"

"You are a healer," she stated with confidence.

"Me, a healer? You mean like you?" I felt confused. *Weren't her gifts natural and God-given? How can I be a healer?*

She continued, "You were led here by God. Our alignment was not superficial. You are meant to do healing work in world service. Do you not know this?"

"World service?" I didn't know what that meant. "My goal is to be a human resource director."

"Well, you will see in time, you are here to learn how to be a healer. Through healing your own illness and experiences you will heal others." She smiled and led me to the door to exit.

Sitting in my car and reflecting, I wondered about where my life was headed. Wasn't I in control of the job I desired? I'd followed intuitive guidance thus far, and believed I was on the right track. Clarity was not present regarding the healer's words. Perhaps desire and intrigue certainly were. Excitement rushed through my body, along with tremendous self-doubt. I drove away, returning to dreams of being a human resource director.

Soul Work Begins

I graduated from college in June 1996, and Lou and I were married in August. I swiftly climbed the ladder toward being a human resource director, which was my dream job. It seemed God was paving the way easily as I was hired by one prestigious company after another. Prior management experience gave me an edge that newly graduated students didn't have. Within less than two years, I was recruiting and searching for a management position.

I now worked as a recruiter for John Hancock Insurance and loved it. One day while sitting at my desk, the voice spoke, "*Quit your job.*" I turned to look behind me as the voice sounded like it was in the same room. No one was present. *Quit my job? Who is telling me to quit my job? And why?* I was busy setting up interviews and ignored the irrational thought.

Two weeks later, the voice spoke again, "*Quit your job.*" Again I turned to see if someone was standing behind me as the voice sounded like it spoke directly into my ear. This time the voice was demanding and strong, as if there were no bargaining to be had.

Without any logical thought process or time to decide what to do, I walked into my boss's office and gave two-weeks' notice. It was not I who walked into the office of my superior and gave notice. I was there in body, but another spirit did the walking and talking. It was my Soul.

After quitting my job I wondered, *Why did I do that? Ah yes! Maybe it's time to look for another job. It's time to step up the ladder again.* Or so I thought. I interviewed for several weeks resulting in no job offers. This made no sense. Whenever God spoke to me in the past, He delivered. Why not now?

By autumn, 1998, Lou and I owned a lovely home. I decided to enjoy the festive time of year and make a decision in the new year as to what my next step was. Dreams of herbal medicine flooded my nighttime space. One morning I awoke and thought, *It's time to start studying herbal medicine for certification.* Becoming a master herbalist was now the new curriculum for the next three years.

Leaving behind dreams of being a human resource director, my Soul path emerged.

Touched by an Angel

In the 1990s people began to acknowledge that angels were among us. Finding a white feather at your doorstep or in an odd place was a sign that an angel was near. Angel books, music, cards, candles, place mats, and mugs were available to accessorize the home. For many of us, this was the first spiritual movement toward acceptance that we are not alone and that loving angels and guides are with us. The TV show *Touched by an Angel* proved to be a big hit as our minds opened to the idea that angels and God love and watch over us. Everyone I knew was talking about seeing white feathers in their daily routines. It was an exciting time as more people began to realize that angels, guides, and God were closer than we previously thought.

Proudly I had my share of white feather sightings; I saw them everywhere. It was the most comforting feeling to know that an angel was looking over my shoulder. One day the angel realm decided to show me just how much it was paying attention to little old me.

Lou and I chose to vacation in Montauk every summer. Long Island's eastern tip was like paradise. The white sandy beaches were pristine, and the energy of this sought-after vacation spot was calming, peaceful, and exuded beauty everywhere. Inlets provided local fishermen access to the deep bluish-green waters of the Atlantic Ocean. Waterfront restaurants offered an exquisite view of land, sea, and air.

One lazy summer day in August, 1999, we sat on the beach and soaked up the healing rays of the warm summer sun. The sky was clear blue, with only a few puffy white clouds scattered about. A cooler packed with water and fruit separated our neatly arranged sand chairs. Lou was deeply engrossed in one of his books on the Civil War, the Alamo, or Chief Crazy Horse. I presumed he enjoyed reading those books as a way to relive many historical past lives in which he was a part.

I gazed at the ocean, eyeing the waves that crashed against the shore only to recede again. Mother Nature is amazing as she tirelessly performs her daily duties. Watching the repetitive manner in which the ocean waves effortlessly flowed in and out was mesmerizing and symbolic of how the flow of life can be just that simple. My mind wandered to an issue we were struggling with at the time, whether or not we were meant to have children.

Obsessive thoughts circled in my mind like an out of control merry-go-round. Should we have children? Why do we or anyone even want children? Why does anyone *not* want children? I closed my eyes, trying to let go of overthinking the subject. A few deep breaths in and out helped to subdue the neurotic thoughts.

My mind calmed as I moved my focus to my breath. Observing how the body effortlessly allows the breath to flow in and out of the lungs relaxed an obsessive mind. After what seemed like ten minutes but was actually about thirty minutes, I opened my eyes and glanced at the sky. To my astonishment, the clear blue sky was saturated with a fleet of white puffy clouds formed in the shape of angels! I blinked a few times to make sure it was not a hallucination. *Where did these clouds come from?* I wondered. They seemed to appear out of nowhere. One big angel cloud in the center was surrounded by at least twenty to thirty little angel clouds. Rays of sunshine shone through the portrait of angels in the sky, illuminating the beach perfectly through the spaces between each cloud. The vision was flawless!

I feverishly poked Lou on his shoulder, disturbing his book reading and taking him out of the battle in American history he was immersed in. Lou was drawn to read about the many battles that occurred on this soil. He had several past lives as an Indian warrior, and another past life as a lone pioneer exploring the rugged terrain of the wilderness. Currently, he was engrossed in the battle fought between Lakota, Chief Crazy Horse, and the U.S. Army under General Custer. I believed reading about these battles was healing him on some level as his Soul remembered the scenes he lived and died though.

Pointing at the sky, I exclaimed, "Look at the sky! Am I seeing things, or have the clouds formed into angel shapes?"

Looking up, he said in his naturally Zen matter-of-fact manner, "The clouds certainly do look like angel shapes." He saw it as clearly as I did! The logical, level-headed man sitting next to me spoke the truth. His testament was the validation I needed to be assured it was not an illusion.

Could anyone else on the beach see the masterpiece of angels in the sky? I wondered. Observing other beach lovers, I noticed that they were not paying attention to what was happening above their heads. They were busy soaking in the sun, swimming, playing in the sand, or overseeing their children. I questioned, *Is this image given specifically for me?* It seemed so. Feeling overwhelmed, my body sank into the back of the sand chair. A few tears rolled down the side of my face as my heart opened to the emotions of love and joy. The miraculous vision in the sky was for me. Again, the metaphysical world was making itself known. Lou immediately returned to his battle.

Within a few minutes the angel clouds began to distort and lose their divine shape. I watched closely as they slowly separated and returned to the usual abstract appearance of cloud formations. Then they disappeared, leaving a clear blue cloudless sky once again. Although the angel clouds were gone, what remained was an intangible feeling of support and love. The feeling of being a significant part of life on Earth rushed through my body. We are never as small or insignificant as we think we are.

Is it really possible that we humans can receive such special gifts from angels, guides, and God? The metaphysical world is grand. It's much bigger than us, yet they care about our well-being. We do matter to them. Could little old me be considered a significant part of the human experience? In truth, every person plays a significant role in life on Earth. Not one person is insignificant in his or her existence. All we need to do is start paying attention, and the nonphysical world will appear and guide us toward our Soul's fulfilment.

No words could describe the magnificence and power of that moment. No specific message was given at that time, but one thing was certain: My trust in the connection to the spirit world was strengthening. I was being shown the way.

Tarot Reader

I was introduced to a wonderful psychic medium who used tarot cards to read the future. On meeting her I felt an instant connection. She lived in Connecticut, and since I lived in New York, I traveled quite a distance to see her. She came highly recommended.

I rang the bell. The door swung open immediately, as if she had intuited my arrival. "Come in, Pauline. It's nice to meet you. How was the drive up here?" Her eyes looked straight into mine, holding a stare. A chill ran down my spine.

"Nice meeting with you as well. The drive was long." I chuckled as I glanced away from her stare. "You live in the deep woods," I added, "so it wasn't easy to find you. But I'm glad I did."

"We readers need certain conditions around us to stay connected to nature. It helps us read more clearly. The trees give me energy," she said.

Something about the explanation of trees created a feeling of joy within me. I had never thought too much about trees, but her comment sparked an innate wisdom about nature.

We sat at her kitchen table. She closed her eyes and mumbled some words that sounded like a prayer of sorts. Then she opened her eyes and began to shuffle the cards.

"Do you know who Edgar Cayce is?" she asked.

"No, I don't," I replied.

"You need to read his books and study his teachings. There's information in his books that you must learn. It's about energy healing and more."

After a moment, she began to tell me her story. "Years ago I was a smoker and developed a cough. So I went to the doctor, who did an X-ray of my chest and found small spots of cancer. The doctor was alarmed and said we must start radiation immediately. I asked how much time I had before actually starting treatment. He told me I hadn't much time, maybe one month. But he added that he wouldn't suggest waiting that long. I told him I'd be back in thirty days."

I leaned in, intrigued.

"Several times a day I meditated on those spots, one at a time. I envisioned them getting smaller and smaller, until they disappeared. In one month I returned to the doctor and requested another X-ray. You know doctors like to be in control, and at first he said no, we must start treatment right away. But I convinced him to do the X-ray anyway. He finally agreed. The film indicated a reduction of the cancerous spots. The doctor was flabbergasted!"

She laughed loudly and continued. "He asked what I had been doing. I told him I meditated several times a day, connected with nature, and envisioned the spots dissolving. He didn't believe me."

My jaw dropped as I continued to listen, anxiously wanting to hear the result.

"I told him I'd be back in another month for a third X-ray. For the next thirty days, I continued my healing routine. When I returned to the doctor, the new X-ray indicated yet another reduction of cancerous spots. Long story short, a month later I returned for a fourth X-ray, and all the spots were gone."

"How did that happen?" I asked in total awe.

She snickered. "The power of our mind is quite strong when we know how to use it properly. It's all about energy. You will learn this."

Her words were so profound, I couldn't receive them. I questioned if I could ever have such an extraordinary ability. She was the second person to advise me about the future as some kind of healer, or energy worker.

The tarot reading itself was insightful, giving me answers to many questions and opening up many more. But the most important thing about our meeting was a fated connection and my introduction to Edgar Cayce, who would go on to be a person of great influence in my life.

And then, of course, there were the trees. Somehow the drive home didn't seem as long as I was now open to the energy of this gift from nature.

Medium 1

One year later I met a psychic medium and decided to have a reading by him. He was a young, gifted medium with a beautiful Irish brogue. My intention for this reading was to contact my father. We sat around a small table in his home. He closed his eyes and sat in silence for a few moments. I felt nervous, not knowing what he would predict. His eyes opened as he spoke with confidence, "You have a spirit guide around you. She is Asian, and she is telling me that her name is Angelica."

"Oh my goodness! Angelica? I've been calling her Delica."

The medium looked hard at me. "She is saying her name is Angelica."

Feeling guilty I hadn't trusted my first impression, I asked, "How do you know this?"

The young medium replied, "She is here. I can see her. And I'm a medium, remember?"

"Yes, of course you would know," I bashfully responded. His knowing needed no further explanation. It was true. I should have trusted my first impression of the name Angelica.

The medium spoke again, "Do you have red chairs in your home?"

Immediately I thought, *How could he know I have two red chairs?* I felt excited knowing a stranger knew little details about my life. I hoped he would reveal information about why I had come to see him. With anticipation I replied, "Yes, there are two red chairs in my living room."

"Your father likes to sit in the red chair closest to the window or glass door. He says he helped you get this home. There's something about it that is familiar. Does this make sense?"

I felt excited by the accuracy of the information. What else would he reveal? Dad must be speaking with him. I wished I could hear my dad. What a gift this young man had! It seemed Dad enjoyed sitting in the living room of my new home. I was comforted by hearing this. I wanted to hear more!

"Yes, it makes perfect sense. I have two red chairs in the living room next to the patio door leading out to the deck. My father lived on a dead-end street, and my home is also on a dead end."

Staring upward as if looking up into space, he paused and then said, "I smell the sea."

Tears flooded my eyes. "My father loved the sea and his boat when he was alive. The sea was his passion and first love." I wiped my cheek as I recalled how much fun we had during the summer months when we pretended to navigate the open seas.

"He is wearing a black captain's hat."

Quickly responding to the accuracy of his visions, I blurted, "He always wore a black captain's hat and loved acting like the captain of his ship.

He'd often joke about how a captain must go down with his ship." I smiled through the tears.

The scene switched in the medium's inner vision. "He is also showing me his legs. He is saying that he has both his legs now. Does this make any sense to you?"

I was overwhelmed with joy as I'd never had a reading reveal such truth and validation that we can communicate with our deceased loved ones quite easily. "Oh, my goodness, yes. When my father was six years old, he was hit by a truck and lost one of his legs. He wore a prosthesis."

"Well he is saying that now he has both his legs. The scars have healed and are completely gone."

I felt overjoyed for him and imagined the vision of his body being completely whole.

"Your father is calling you his 'shining star.'"

On hearing those words, my heart skipped a beat, my body sunk into the chair, and I started weeping, remembering the moment my father and I shared when we danced to Frank Sinatra's "Summer Wind." Feelings of love rushed through my body as I relived the vision of us dancing together. It was one of the happiest moments of my life. It occurred to me that my father was still with me, guiding and protecting me from above. I was comforted by this information.

The medium went on to tell me many things about my father when he was alive. There was no doubt at all that the medium connected with my father in heaven. The sequence of these events validated that the connection between humans and spirit is just a belief away.

Transcendental Meditation

Since the early 1980s I had wanted to learn how to meditate using Transcendental Meditation (TM). In 1999 the opportunity finally appeared. One spot was available for the upcoming weekend training, which was only four days away. I presumed this spot was for me. Finally, a long-awaited desire was about to come true! Gleefully thanking God for the opportunity, I wrote out a check, stashed it in my wallet, and anxiously waited for Saturday to arrive.

Walking into the home of the meditation teacher, I felt anxious and wondered, *Can I honestly learn to meditate? Isn't meditation for gurus?* We were a group of six students sitting in the living room of a trained TM teacher, who was a gifted teacher of the Maharishi Center in Iowa. *Wow,* I thought, *this is incredible, and real!*

After two days of training and practicing TM twice daily for twenty minutes, the instructor asked if anyone had noticed any type of change in their behaviors, emotions, or physical conditions. For many years it had been normal for me to wake up in the middle of the night to urinate. Then I realized I hadn't woken up at night in two days. Excited to reveal my improvement, I raised my hand to answer, "I stopped peeing in the middle of the night." The group laughed, but it was true.

Very encouraged by my report, the instructor explained how meditation is a self-healing tool. With regular practice we have the ability to heal ourselves of many physical and emotional conditions. One woman had Tourette syndrome and noticed the nervous twitching associated with her condition had slightly subsided. We were all so happy for her. At the time I didn't realize how powerful meditation could be. Soon I began to accept how the power of the mind profoundly heals the body.

Medium 2

In 2000 I was introduced to a different kind of medium, Asandra. She did not speak to the dead. Her gift was to allow a spirit guide to speak through her, so a person could communicate directly with his or her guide. This medium was a trance channel for spirit. Before working with someone, Asandra would determine through a short phone interview if a reading to contact your spirit guide through her was appropriate. I felt Angelica was leaving me now, yet another spirit entity was close by. Not being able to get a sense of who this spirit guide was on my own, the Universe wisely sent me someone who could help. The first phone session with the medium broadened the course of my life.

Initially, Asandra did a general reading on what she saw for the next three-to-six-year cycle of my life. She spoke about cycles of energy and used the analogy of waves crashing on the shore and then receding. I remembered that exact vision a few years back, while vacationing in Montauk. The symbolism felt right to me.

The medium explained the specific events and life-changes that would be part of my life. At the time, I did not understand most of what she foretold, despite the beautiful way in which she spoke. My concern was to know who my guide was, to find out more about creating an herbal practice, and about possibly having a child. After ten minutes of sharing her visions, she explained that she would now go into a trancelike state to channel my guide. During this time she allowed spirit to completely take over her body, removing herself.

This meant she would not be present, interfere, control, or remember any information that was revealed.

Nervousness and anticipation filled my heart, causing it to beat rapidly. I took a few deep breaths in and out to try to relax.

The medium went into trance, and then out of her mouth came a voice that was different from just a moment ago. But it wasn't just the timbre of her voice that changed. Her grammar and use of language were different. It felt unique and specific, like it was just for me.

My new guide, Heshtar, greeted me with a beautiful welcome in a way I had never heard before. Her words were soft and exuded loving, supportive energy. "Greetings, and welcome, dear blessed Soul. I am Heshtar, your master guide."

These were some of the most beautiful words I'd ever heard. I was so affected I did not know how to respond. No one ever called me a blessed Soul. The feeling from such words were divine, I could not receive them, but the yearning to embrace them was strong. She took my breath away by the love I felt pouring through the phone line.

Heshtar explained that she would now be my main guide, along with many other spirit entities. The spirit entity went on to say that by allowing myself to be guided for many years and healing my life, I had attracted her. Apparently I was now ready to know her and the new guidance that would be imparted now and in the future. The master went on to tell me about who I was as a Soul being and that through the awakening process, I would come to understand my Soul's true purpose on Earth. The master guide foretold the future of my life and explained that I would be a part of many Souls on Earth, thereby contributing to the evolution of human consciousness. She explained that my path would show me how to release the constraints and limitations of human life and that I would teach others how to live in a more enlightened way. The process of awakening would take many years, and I must initially keep choosing it before my mind could naturally grasp higher levels of consciousness and maintain such a level. The enlightened being explained that I was here now to awaken to my role, my participation in the evolution of human consciousness. The way in which I would bring this consciousness to others with excitement and inspiration would be through my own experiences. This path would bring me into an entirely new life. Then she asked if I had any questions or concerns.

The power of the master guide was intimidating. I was silent, stunned, perhaps a bit in shock on hearing this information. What questions or concerns could I possibly have, given the fact that my mind did not grasp one word of the beautiful dissertation spoken by the voice of this spirit? These words were far more complex than just, "Give yourself time." I did not know what to say. How does a person respond to such profound guidance? Me, contributing to evolution and assisting in the awakening of human consciousness? At the time, I did not understand. All I wanted was an herbal practice and maybe a child. I remembered the words of the healer indicating that I would help people heal in the future. I felt like Dorothy speaking to the Great and Powerful Oz.

I needed to say something. "Welcome, and thank you for coming," was all I could come up with in a timid voice. "May I ask if I'm going to create an herbal healing practice?"

The master guide spoke, "Do you want an herbal healing practice?"

"Well, yes, very much so."

"Then why wouldn't you have it?" the guide responded.

She returned the responsibility to me regarding what I wanted. In that moment I realized what she was actually saying was, if you really want something, why wouldn't you have it? The responsibility to create anything that is of Soul desire resides completely within us. I was beginning to receive that message loud and clear.

I proceeded to ask the next question. "Should I have a child?"

"Why do you want a child?"

Replying shyly, as I was a bit stunned by her response, I said, "Why?" Then I answered, "Because I believe I'd be a wonderful mother."

She spoke in a most loving tone. "Dear one, there will be children in your life. And if not from your body, there will be many whom you will love as your own."

While the message was transmitted with words of love, I didn't quite understand. Not wanting to push the issue, we moved on to other areas of curiosity.

About six months later, another trance session revealed I had an archangel assigned to me who would offer protection and guidance. Angels are without gender, and the name was Willow. Willow spoke through the medium in a voice that was again completely different. The cherub sounded childlike and playful, just as we might imagine a child to be. Shortly thereafter, a sweet kitten came into our lives. We named her Willow.

Energy Medicine

While studying herbal medicine and practicing TM, I searched for energy classes to begin to understand how energy, emotions, thoughts, and life experiences played a role in illness, wellness, intuition, and purpose.

A new world was again opening up. Thirty years ago, energy medicine was unheard of; however, when God places you on a destiny path, what you need is given.

I started my journey toward becoming certified in many energy modalities, such as subtle energy body healing, Reiki Master, Thought Field Therapy, and Light Body Healing. I also studied metaphysics. The new medicine made sense to me, more so than traditional medicine. Getting to the root cause of an issue and healing the energy of it, is the only way to truly heal.

The first energy class in a series of three was learning about subtle energy systems. It was located in Warwick, New York, ninety minutes from my home. I wasn't accustomed to driving long distances at the time and asked Lou to drive with me in separate cars to assure arriving safely in the remote location. We drove through mountains and winding roads to arrive at the Peach Grove Inn B&B, where I stayed during the three-day class. The building was charming, with an old-world cottage feel to it. We were greeted by a husband and wife couple, probably in their late fifties, wearing big smiles.

"There's tea and biscuits in the living room if you are inclined to join us," said the husband.

His wife escorted us to our lovely room filled with antiques and heavy patchwork quilts for warmth. Lou stayed overnight and left in the morning, after breakfast. I headed over to the teacher's home to attend class.

In the first subtle energy class, the teacher scanned all the student's energy fields and offered an insight into what she saw metaphysically. When it was my turn to be scanned, I was a slightly nervous. *What will she see?* I wondered. Her eyes scanned my body. At first I thought she was physically looking me up and down in judgment. Insecurities arose within and I thought, *Am I good enough to do this? Do I really want to be here?*

Then she smiled and said, "You have fairies in your aura. They are flittering all around. Do you know this?"

"No, I didn't know that! But I totally believe in fairies." I was happy with her insight.

"What do you do with the earth?" she asked.

"I'm studying herbal medicine, and I'm an earth sign, Capricorn, who loves to garden."

"Well that's why you've got fairy friends in your aura. They help you in many ways, including tending your garden."

I felt so excited I wanted to loudly burst out and say, "I'm a fairy godmother!" Instead I said, "How wonderful! Thank you for telling me. I wish I could see the little creatures."

From that day forward, whenever I gardened I'd call to my fairy friends to join me. Sometimes I thought they were giggling and swooping around me as I felt twinges on exposed parts of my body, such as head, arms, or legs. Sometimes it felt like a gnat bite, but there was no physical indication of a bite. I assumed it was the fairies having fun with me since being acknowledged.

After class I arrived back at the B&B around five o'clock in the evening to the scent of cinnamon scones baking in the oven. I tiptoed into the kitchen to have a look-see.

"Come in, Pauline. Would you like a cup of tea and a scone?" offered the Innkeeper.

"That would be wonderful. I've just taken my first energy class, and my head is spinning. I'm starved!"

She looked at me and smiled when I realized she probably didn't understand what I was talking about. Very few people were open to understanding the metaphysical world. We sat at the kitchen table and chatted. She was honest and shared how much she loved her business and welcomed people into her home.

"I'd like to increase my business somehow," she said. I listened.

At the end of the three days I felt in deep gratitude for the owners of the Peach Grove Inn, which kept me safe and in a small degree of luxury while being away from home. I loved this little place and couldn't wait to return. "I'll be back in a few months, when the next energy class is scheduled," I said as I walked out of the building and packed my bag into the car.

"We look forward to seeing you again," she smiled and waved goodbye.

Then I looked at the sweet, charming cottage and envisioned a beautiful white light of abundance around it. "God, she is a good woman who is kind and generous. May she and her husband prosper to their hearts' content, Amen." I spoke in a soft whisper. Opening the door and settling into the driver's seat for the drive home, I felt peaceful and excited about the new skills I had learned.

Months later, when I returned, the owner and I sat once again in her kitchen sipping on tea and enjoying freshly baked goods. "You know, I don't know what happened, but we've been so busy here at the Inn I can hardly keep up!" Her eyes were wide with excitement.

"I'm happy to hear this wonderful news for you and your husband!

What's not to love about the Peach Grove Inn?" I said taking a bite of the delicious cinnamon scone. I remembered the prayer to God to provide abundance to this haven. And so it was done. I felt overjoyed for them.

We can ask God for abundance for others. Since we haven't been taught to ask for ourselves, others can ask for us. When we are open to receive, and apparently the owners of the Peach Grove Inn were unknowingly open to receive, abundance will be given from the heavens. At the Soul level, we are meant to live in abundance and nothing less.

A new way of life commenced. Instead of feeling powerless over how life was unfolding or if my health would continue to improve, soon small bursts of confidence emerged with the understanding of the degree of control I had over myself.

Soon after, I took a weeklong class in New York City to learn about mind-body integration. Our group of twenty-five students sat in a circle learning how to tap into the energy of our minds and bodies. After one exercise, the teacher asked us to pair up. I had observed a powerful woman named Margaret and desired to work with her. Instantly, I looked across the room and thought, *I'd like to work with Margaret.* Two seconds later, Margaret turned to look at me, and walked over to where I was standing.

"You wish to work with me?" she asked.

"Yes! I was just thinking that. How did you know?" I was shocked.

"I have a tendency to hear people's thoughts. Then, I looked over at you, indicating the thought came from you. Very well then, let's work together."

I was astounded by this telepathic ability and excited to have the opportunity to work with her. I hoped I might absorb some of her telepathic ability. I was in awe.

Shortly thereafter, I experienced a telepathic conversation with my friend Cindy. Cindy was a healer in the making, as I was. We met at a workshop hosted by an internationally acclaimed energy healer, Rosalyn Bruyere, a pioneer in the field of energy medicine. At the time I needed someone who understood the path of spiritual awakening in my life. The community of awakening Souls was tiny, and I longed for a friend and colleague. I asked God to bring such a person into my life. At first glance I knew Cindy was authentic, and aside from learning energy medicine, apparently she was one of the reasons I felt guided to attend this workshop. We became friends instantly and felt we were cut from the same cloth.

One day while lying in bed resting, Cindy's voice popped into my head, and a dialogue began. *I think I need to get off this medication I'm on.*

Telepathically I replied, *The medication seems to be causing intestinal upset. What about using herbs instead?*

I'm not sure which herbs to use or if they are safe. Her thoughts merged with mine.

I can help you with herbal medicine. Are you ready to try it?

The dialogue ended, and I wondered if it was real. Later that day Cindy called me. "I want to get off this medicine, and I'm thinking about trying herbal medicine."

"Jesus, Cindy! We must have had some kind of telepathic conversation because I told you to get off the medication, and I'd help you with herbal remedies!"

"You know, I felt like some kind of communication was happening. But I wasn't sure it was real because I was driving."

We agreed the conversation through our thoughts was indeed real. It was a powerful moment in which we both began to realize the innate power of the Soul.

Our views of life are limited by the human conditions of fear, control, illusion, and ego insecurities. We have never been taught about who we are or what our true purposes are. Nor do we have an understanding about who we are as Soul beings until we become curious enough to explore the metaphysical world. We must take steps to reunite with the natural world of spirit and elementals, such as fairies, angels, and spirit entities. We must connect with Mother

Earth, the trees, flowers, and the elements of air, water, fire, and earth to understand how energy profoundly affects our lives. Your Soul yearns to walk its authentic path, which will look nothing like you imagine. This path can't be planned or figured out logically.

The journey toward healing and awakening is lifelong, requiring dedication and desire. But I assure you, this is the greatest journey of all.

Experiences with angels, guides, mediums, and God were profound. Life started to change in ways I had never imagined. Curiosity about the metaphysical world was growing. This triggered a deeper exploration into spirituality, energy, and consciousness. The experiences that the Universe brought forth could not be ignored or left unexplored. To brush these experiences off as not being significant to some greater purpose, would be total ignorance. The connection between worlds was growing stronger, and in truth, I was thrilled about it! I felt as if I was connecting to the mystery of life. And in many ways, I was.

Shortly thereafter God delivered an herbal healing practice. It simply came into existence, and before I knew it, I was set up as an herbalist and emerging energy healer. The small spare bedroom in our home was converted into a healing room, painted in pale-blue walls with white furniture accents. I hung pictures of angels and fairies. Statues symbolic of higher consciousness, such as dolphins, The Blessed Mother, and Buddha, were placed on the white desk and corner wicker cabinet to aid in healing.

I began to explore essential oils and crystals. Visits to a local metaphysical store, where I purchased crystals, was enchanting. Certain crystals seemed to jump out at me as if to say, "Take me home! I'm your crystal!" Clients came through word of mouth, and my practice grew. Fairies surely joined in healing sessions for would-be mothers to safeguard a growing fetus. These little elementals flittered around in my aura. And at times clients could feel the tiny creatures poking around their bodies, assisting in releasing energy blockages. In particular, I was drawn to crystal wands. Selenite and Kyanite were my favorites to clear unwanted energy. The newly created room became known as, the little blue healing room. Upon walking into this room, a person would often feel a vibrational shift into peace. The Universe was leading the way as I kept looking inward and upward.

Conclusion: Listen carefully to the delicate whisper of spirit; trust you're being led home. Trust in your intuition; it has your highest future in mind. You are never alone.

Chapter 6

From Shadow into Light

How can you say to your brother, "Brother, let me take the speck out of your eye," when you yourself fail to see the plank in your own eye? You hypocrite, first take the plank out of your eye, and then you will see clearly to remove the speck from your brother's eye.

Luke 6:42 (NIV)

A New Paradigm Emerges

By ignoring our shadow side we only contribute to the ignorance of not knowing the light within us. The shadow or light patterns within the conscious and subconscious mind are what create our external lives. Don't be afraid to explore your inner world, change it, clean it up, do whatever it takes to make it whole. Then witness miracles occur in your life. Every unfolding experience is an opportunity to grow, heal, or move beyond something outworn. Without judgment, these experiences can be seen as divine growth spurts to aid in the awakening of the Soul.

September 11, 2001, changed the world. Prior to that day, the collective was sleeping, so to speak. Very few individuals were awakened or aware of the spirit world. It was time for a great awakening. On that day everyone was shaken to the core. For many individuals, it was their wake-up call through an event that was karmically scripted into our history. It was destined to occur. At the end of 2000, my master guide said, "In the coming year, dear one, you will be very grateful for all that you have." At that time I didn't understand what I would be grateful for but trusted the message to be true.

As the day unfolded I felt the terror of everyone in the world, including myself. I remembered what the master guide had said. But being grateful now wasn't about getting a new car or anything physical. It was about life and death.

My brother worked near the World Trade Center, and after the towers fell our family was panicked about his whereabouts. Phone lines were jammed or not in service as we all tried to reach him, desperately hoping he was not harmed. Somehow I knew my brother was safe, but I couldn't trust my feelings without confirmation; so I, too, panicked.

By some miracle Lou and my brother connected by phone. Lou's office was on the outskirts of the city. He left a message on my brother's office phone and instructed him to walk many miles from downtown New York City up toward the 59th Street Bridge and cross over it into Long Island City, where a vehicle would be waiting for him. My brother, along with many other people, walked through the dust-ridden city toward safety. When he arrived on the outskirts of the city, Lou called to confirm his safety. I immediately called my mother and sister-in-law to ease their worry. We all broke down and cried in relief. Indeed, there was much to be grateful for.

Others were not so fortunate. A husband and wife who lived a few houses down the block from ours never came home that evening. My husband's friend lost his son. Several of my clients witnessed individuals jump out of buildings to their deaths. This was a crisis so huge we were stunned into opening our eyes to many realities. Were we to stay in fear and hate? Or rise above it through awakening?

This karmic day was not only one of humankind's biggest tragedies. The shattering day brought forth a new dimension of reality, the fourth dimension. This new dimension was to be anchored into the ego-oriented third-dimensional plane of selfishness, greed, manipulation, control, and physical material obsession. A new dimension arrived to assist those who were ready to awaken to the spirit world, a dream world of magic, transformation, intuition, psychic awareness, and healing lifetimes of karma. Anchoring in the fourth dimension split the world's aura open like a walnut shell, spewing darkness that would be our catalyst to awaken the Soul. Fourth- dimensional nonphysical energy and Soul awareness were descending upon us, slithering in through opened cracks of humanity's ego wounds. Ironically, this day fostered a crystal clear blue sky and shining sun offering perfect September weather.

In the following twenty years, thousands of healers, intuitive, and psychic mediums emerged around the planet. Being in service to the world and creating unity was a new theme from the self-centered material world. Many would-be healers were connected to this point in time to awaken their Souls' contracts with God and Earth, to bring in a new cycle of fourth-dimensional energy for the collective mind. We would remain quiet, in transformation for many years until the masses were ready to accept spirituality with all its metaphysical gifts as a valid method for evolution, being healthy, happy, and abundant. We would wait for God's timing to begin speaking more publicly about our true Soul nature, teaching about energy healing, and healing many people who believed this was possible.

Curiosity grew rapidly as healers healed themselves and offered services to others. This time represented only the conception stage of awakening. But as with any new endeavor, the seed must be planted. Perhaps now we might truly learn how to open our minds, hearts, and Souls to ourselves, each other, and life as God would have it. Through a massive world crisis came compassion, unity, love, and fear.

The sleeping world's normal life splintered on that fateful day. So did my heart. Three weeks later, I succumbed to an illness no doctor, healer, or herb could cure. My body was plagued with a strange flu. I was exhausted with flu-like symptoms, yet I wasn't really sick. I called the healer.

"You've gone into transformation, Pauline," she explained.

"Transformation? What do you mean?" With so many years of healing, I couldn't imagine what else needed to be healed. The ignorance of the ego mind was speaking.

"Your symptoms are flu-like, but what's really happening is you are in a massive purge."

"A massive purge? What is that, and how long will this last?"

She explained further in a matter-of-fact tone, "You are healing at a very deep level. The energies of life's circumstances are being released from your energy system. You'll be in transition for about five to seven years before you will be clear."

"What?" I exclaimed. "Five to seven years of illness? Oh my God, that's not possible. How will I function? Will I be able to celebrate holidays? Go on vacation?" I was frantic. I couldn't bear the thought of being ill again. I feared it so.

Chuckling, the healer replied, "No, you won't be ill at all, but you will be transforming from the old self into the new self. You will need to rest, and to learn how to meet your own needs."

Relieved I would not be ill but still curious what would happen during these years of transformation, I asked, "What do you mean transforming the old self into the new self? What should I expect?"

"You just have to go through it. Your inner being is changing. You're waking up! You'll see." We hung up the phone. The vague conversation provided just enough information to settle my fears.

Her words relating to an inner being sparked deeper curiosity. Each day was to be lived moment by moment. Approximately two months passed before my health was restored. I was grateful for the return of wellness by Christmas. However, I was not the same Pauline as a few months before. Something inside me had changed.

Graceful Isolation, 2001–2008

> Pain is only triggered by another person when there is already pain within you. (Roman, *Personal Power through Awareness*, p. 115)

Connection to my all my spirit guides strengthened. New spirit guides showed up as I continued to awaken. These new spirits made themselves known through my intuitive sense. I began to sense their energy and each one was slightly different.

A unique transformation began to occur. Once again, something inside me began to churn, and intuitively I knew it was time to look deeper into my wounds, insecurities, and fears. At first I rejected the notion to look deeper. However, suppressed feelings connected to childhood, adolescence, adulthood, and karmic ego-patterns were smoldering underneath. Stuffing down the depths of my inner world was no longer possible. In that moment, I began to see why humans do what we do, why we hurt and manipulate each other, and why we live in tremendous lack of love, prosperity, health, peace, and compassion while fostering survival fear as a basic foundation for life.

To heal deeply I had to become an observer of myself while not judging or taking the wounds too seriously. Wounds are natural to human life, yet they do not represent the Soul's essence. Maintaining some level of humor about what I found internally was helpful. Learning to laugh at myself with love was necessary. The time had come to dig into the long-awaited Sweet, Sour, Salty hereditary patterns, including every wound I pretended didn't exist.

From this awareness I was thrust into seven years of graceful isolation, where the focus of my life was to heal the fragmented, wounded parts of myself. I was being shown how to be selfish in a healthy way.

In times of being alone, I learned about who I was and who I was becoming. At times I was tired and couldn't sleep. Downloads of energy ran through my body several times a day, imparting new thoughts and insights. Hot or cool flashes ran through my flesh and bones, causing profuse sweating or chills. Often times, deep purges of energy created tremendous physical pain in my body. Massage, acupuncture and using my own energy skills helped to release the painful energy. The hips, lower back, and legs seemed to be the areas where pain surfaced the most.

Then, there were the headaches. I was not a person to experience headaches, but I began to experience what some people would call a migraine, yet I knew it wasn't a migraine. It was a severe energy blockage around the head and neck area. Usually, massaging the sore spots on the head, and neck with lavender oil helped relieve the discomfort. Meditating or resting also helped, however, bouts of insomnia returned. Every day was a surprise as to what I would experience. I learned to go with the flow of each day and addressed symptoms as they occurred.

I felt like I had gone backwards into ill health, but that wasn't the case. I remembered the comforting words of the healer explaining that I just needed to go through this. My body needed rest, yet once evening arrived, I'd often feel an internal buzzing, like an electrical current flowing through me, and it was. Higher vibrations of universal life-force energy began to flow through my organs, cells, bones, and blood.

New worlds were opening up, and I needed space to explore them without distraction. At first it was challenging to be alone, but then I quickly valued this time and found that most of my spiritual growth occurred during my solitary time in silence. I needed the outside world to go away, so I could explore my inner world.

Some of the most powerful, eye-opening revelations occurred during this phase. Those moments allowed clarity and inspiration to awaken. New information downloaded into my mind from the Universe as I cocooned from the external world. Never did I feel lonely while in the presence of spirit. The truth was, I felt loved, whole, and nurtured in a way that no human being had ever provided. The ability to self-soothe and nurture my inner child in times of great challenge catapulted the connection to my higher self.

External distractions prevent the desire to travel deep into your inner worlds. Getting caught up in the outside world will not allow healing and awakening at the deepest level, which is where all transformation must occur. If the opinions of those who shaped you live in your daily environment, there's a risk of being pulled back into the old ways of living and thinking. Releasing the need to conform may require some distance from those who want you to remain the same.

How can you see your own truth if you are constantly bombarded with external stimuli telling you how to feel, how to be numb, how to think, how to be, how to dress, how to act, and what to believe? Family and friends will be challenged by your awakening because as you change, they too feel the energetic changes. They may be uncomfortable with it and unconsciously try to distract you from this path. Being able to explain, in a loving way, what is occurring with you might help, depending on how open-minded they are. I experienced a lot of disapproval simply because they did not understand what I was going through. Neither did I understand. As best as possible, I tried to explain the awakening process. I felt compassion for them, yet I continued to follow my path, learning how to release codependence and attachment while reaching higher toward God. It will be very difficult to individuate and awaken your Soul if you are constantly being reminded to conform to who you are not.

Engaging in mundane chores like laundry or housecleaning or

grocery shopping seemed to be the key for me because I considered these to be mindless actions. Engaging in mindless activity was exactly how higher information was able to seep into my expanding consciousness. I actually started to enjoy these activities because at the end of the day, some wisdom had been imparted. The mystery of life was unfolding for which I felt much gratitude. Graceful isolation was one of the biggest gifts I gave myself as orchestrated by God. I accepted it as complete truth and essential.

To feel the energy of spirit around me all day was a profound experience, and spirit is not serious all the time. Sometimes I found myself laughing as spirit showed me the ridiculous behaviors of human beings—of course as it pertained to me. Working through darkness always resulted in feeling more alive, joyful, and loving. Keep in mind that experiencing darkness is not bad; it's a necessary step of the journey into the light.

So glorious it is to be in the company of spirit! It refreshes and recharges the human being like nothing else! Sometimes my spirit guides would show images of what I needed to understand or heal, especially from the past. Other times they spoke softly into the back of my head, which increased my clairaudient ability. Then, images of the future were given, which often startled me as I couldn't quite grasp the expanded version of myself, just yet.

As innate gifts opened up, so did my ability to feel the energy of people around me. I chose to socialize with those whose energy exchanges were positive. Those who drained or manipulated were kept at a distance. We are not supposed to suck life-force energy from others; we are designed to receive it from the Universe through healing, meditation, reconnection to nature, and recognizing the Universe as our source. The Soul is restored in this way. As the intricate connection between God and I grew stronger, relationship boundaries with others became healthier as they were based more on love than control, survival, and fear.

Socializing wasn't appealing. Mundane, gossipy conversation was a turnoff. Healthy detachment from others, especially from family members, was necessary as I began to undo every belief system I learned and then changed them into supportive structures to help me heal, and grow. Family can be the biggest mirror into mental, emotional, and spiritual patterns in need of transformation. Letting go of most of what Mom, Dad, a pastor or rabbi, schoolteacher or coach taught me about how to live was challenging because it was these patterns that contributed to the feelings of being accepted, loved, and part of a community. Breaking free from everything that taught me to be codependent, approved of, insignificant, insecure, or to do the "right thing" —especially when it felt wrong—was necessary to change.

During the summer months, Lou and I were often invited to spend weekends at a friend's home on the sandy beaches of Long Island. As my transformation unfolded, I was guided to refrain from being in large groups of people. One Saturday morning, we were packed and ready to leave our house to head to the beach when a wave of fatigue washed over me. I sat on the couch and couldn't move. I knew what was happening and thought, *oh, it's that time again!* I did, however, need to make a quick decision. Do I serve others and not disappoint them? Or do I serve myself and stay at home?

Lou walked into the living room to find me lying on the couch, "Ready to go?" he asked.

"Lou, I'm sorry. I can't go. I'm exhausted. Being in the company of lots of people would only cause more fatigue. I need to cocoon and stay home, alone. Please go and enjoy yourself. Send my loving regards."

He understood and drove to the beach to enjoy himself. He sent photos of our friends waving to me, the sun glistening over the ocean as it set, and the delicious foods prepared to celebrate life. I rested in the cocoon of God's love as transformation continued.

Wiping the old slate clean was an arduous task but a most rewarding one. I became selfishly healthy as I focused on me. It seemed a veil lifted from my eyes, and suddenly I was able to see deeply into myself and others for the purposes of healing. A love affair with all parts of myself was sprouting.

Several consistent clients remained on the calendar, while new referrals inquired about energy healing. Clients and family are always a healer's best teacher. My trust in God grew as the grace He provided eventually created miraculous cures for clients, but not before complete surrender of my ego desires.

Inner Worlds: Desire, Drive, Ego, Soul

A word about ego. It is your friend in that it helps you to see how disconnected you are from your Soul. We should not want to kill the ego or destroy it; we must transform it into an advocate for self-growth. It matters not how much you transform, only that you begin the process. Your personal transformation is vital to an evolving world and future generations.

Going inward, I was shown various parts of the personality. Spirit showed me how to examine myself in a new way. Within the whole of the personality lived various parts of the self. Three parts of the self were shown in this way: the ego (which I also call the "wounded ego"), inner desire/drive, which creates desire, and pushes us forward, and a beautiful, powerful Soul represented by a blue-white light, which represents divine love. All these aspects are not separate as they comprise the personality as a whole. The ego never stops challenging us, as long as we are human, but it does quiet down and finds a healthier place in life as you heal and ascend on the journey of evolution. Shame is the ego feeling embarrassed about its flaws. As we accept that to err is human, shame can be healed through nonjudgment.

Inner Desire and Drive: Even though I consider inner desire and drive part of the ego structure, it's a part that you want to keep. Without inner desires and drive, you would not want to create anything. So in this case, a little ego is good!

We are innately programmed to aspire to higher goals in life. However, our truest aspirations are to rise into higher realms of consciousness. Our inner drive pushes us to create and to manifest our purpose and life's fulfillments. Everyone has different inner desires. Your Soul is programmed with its truest desires, and one of the deepest desires is to awaken the Soul as this leads to the understanding of innate greatness. True desire is connected to the Soul's purpose as long as it comes from your heart, not your head. True desire and drive are usually focused on contributing to the world in some way, and more importantly, to transform ego into Soul.

There are many ways to contribute to making the world a better place. Still, the truth of what to do and how to do it isn't usually known to the mind. It comes through transformation and an inward connection to the Soul and God. Everyone has a true Soul purpose, and it is not necessarily something you are good at.

Everyone knows what inner desire feels like because we all desire to be happy, healthy, successful, and filled with love. Wanting these things is natural to living abundantly. We spend lots of time and money trying to obtain these desires and be happy, but we often fail or only partially succeed. Why does this happen? The problem lies with a belief system that says it is impossible to have everything you want. The ego is still wounded, insecure, and fearful, and accepts lack as its reality. This is very old paradigm patterning. When the Soul has not yet been awakened, life is created from limited beliefs, fearful thoughts, and insecurities.

Obsessive, controlling desires or the need to accumulate things to feel fulfilled isn't the inner desire of the Soul; it's the ego. Obsession is the ego demon of inner desire connected to lack. It's based on ego mentality: What can I get, and how quickly can I get it? How do I control what I get so I will feel safe, loved and fulfilled?

On the other hand, the Soul is not wounded and is completely fulfilled within itself. The Soul itself is so complete it just wants to be itself. Through the fulfillment of the human/Soul awakening, we learn how to embrace Soul mentality: I am safe. I have everything

I need, and can easily co-create anything else I need. What can I give? How can I help? More on the Soul later.

Wounded Ego: This is the part of us that needs attention, healing, and love as it represents our shadow side. This precious, delicate part of the personality has been born from abuse, hurt, betrayal, deception, manipulation, control, and from not feeling loved, worthy, successful, good enough, smart enough, or attractive enough. Feeling misunderstood by family, friends, government, educators, religious leaders, and the local community also contributes to the development of your shadow side. The wounded ego feels inferior due to ethnic background, ancestral patterns, negative life-circumstances and perceptions of reality. Creating from this part of the ego always leaves us feeling slightly empty and wanting more because the foundation is lack-oriented. Hence the desire to control the outer world to somehow guarantee we get what we want. This aspect is where real transformation is needed.

As my wounded ego transformed, I developed a relationship with my Soul, and that positively affected the relationship with self, others, and every other aspect of my entire life.

Belief Systems

Opening your mind and erasing all your current belief systems will give you a clean slate on which to reinvent positive, higher belief systems based on how you want to live your life. I believe truth of the Soul can't be known until we are ready to release our former belief systems. The belief systems that still serve you will either remain or return with a slightly higher degree of consciousness. Don't adopt another person's beliefs. Instead, explore your conscious and subconscious beliefs, and you will find your truth.

I was shown that changing my belief systems and thoughts (mental body) will expand the mind. If you don't change your belief about something, you won't be able to change your behavior, manifest a dream, or awaken your inner power. Removing beliefs that keep you small and insignificant is the first step. If you believe you will never be healthy because hereditary patterns dictate your health, then you will create disease. If you believe only the rich get richer, then you'll not create your own richness. Essentially, I worked very diligently to erase all lack-oriented beliefs and started over. Of course beliefs set in kindness, unity, and generosity remained stable.

Any dominant trait or belief will need to be changed to a more balanced one that reflects the loving, tolerant, compassionate, wisdom of your higher self. If any of your beliefs are extreme, they will need restructuring because your Soul isn't extreme. It is stable, and loving. Staying away from extreme beliefs would be a good goal to set.

Be constantly open to changing and evolving your belief systems throughout your life. You will find that as you continue to awaken, belief systems that you once thought were new and empowering may need to change over time as well. Transformation will continue to occur as long as you keep choosing it. At some point you will reach a level where transformation happens automatically, without needing to consciously choose it. But this usually takes years of choosing beforehand. Accept that you will always be in a state of shedding the old and embracing the new.

These are some of the beliefs I saw as being necessary to change for myself. Some of these beliefs came from family members, friends, and clients, yet I saw fragments within myself.

Conscious Beliefs	Changed Belief
It's better to give than receive.	I receive abundance without guilt.
It's not good to confront.	I am allowed to confront in a healthy way.
If I work hard, then I will get everything I want.	My Soul co-creates with God everything I need in divine timing.

It's bad to feel angry.	It's okay to feel angry as long as I don't take it out on others. I honor my feelings and release them.
Money is evil.	Money is not evil; it depends on how I earn and use it. I deserve to be prosperous.
I am not pretty enough.	Beauty comes from within, and I am beautiful in all ways.
I am not successful enough.	Success is judged by how I feel about myself. I honor and respect myself.
I need to be rich to feel powerful.	My Soul is rich and powerful in love.
I have difficulty losing weight because it's genetic.	I overcome my genetic patterns. My body maintains a healthy weight through increased metabolism.
I need to be on top to survive.	I trust myself and my life. I create what I need.
People don't change.	People can change if they are willing to do the work.
I am not cut out for greatness.	My Soul is great; therefore I am.
I need a child to be happy and fulfilled.	I am fulfilled by knowing my Soul and God.
I am not good enough.	I am good enough just as I am.
I am not worthy.	I am worthy and lovable.

I am insignificant.	My existence on Earth is significant. I matter.
If I am a good person, then everyone will like me.	If I like me, then I am at peace.
I sabotage my life.	I co-create with God, allowing abundance.
I am a victim.	All experiences help me to be empowered through forgiveness.
I am working hard enough.	I am open to changing how I work to create more prosperity or leisure time.
My religion is superior.	All religions serve some purpose.
I have no power over a disease.	Loving myself will heal all disease. I have the power.
I am afraid to love.	God loves me. It is safe to love and be vulnerable.

Create your own positive beliefs with supportive affirmations or mantras that resonate and touch you deeply. I like the word "mantra" as it reminds me I must repeat it over and over, until the energy of the words shift from the mental body into the emotional body then the physical body. When you begin to feel the emotion of the words, the healing process has begun. As you embody the energy of the words as emotions, your vibration will rise out of lack into the person you want to be. Keep the affirmation or mantra simple, and let the words ring true to your heart and Soul!

Mantra Exercise

Create your mantra. Use the word "grateful," and add an emotion. Gratitude is the foundation for an abundant life. Emotion attracts in the desired result. For example: I am grateful and filled with joy as I create prosperity. Or, I am grateful and filled with love as I create a harmonious relationship.

Once you have created a mantra that rings true, bring it through the chakra system as often as possible every day. Once you're proficient at this, it will take only a few minutes each time. The more you practice, the more quickly your mantra will become a reality. Remember, the mantra must ring true to your Soul, not your ego.

Step 1: Start at the seventh chakra, the crown of your head, in silence. Only think of the mantra.

Step 2: Bring the mantra to the sixth chakra, the third eye, and see the mantra fulfilled in a vision.

Step 3: Bring the mantra to the fifth chakra, the throat, and speak the mantra aloud.

Step 4: Bring the mantra to the fourth chakra, the heart, open your heart and feel the love the mantra brings into your heart.

Step 5: Bring the mantra into the third chakra, the solar plexus, and feel worthy of the mantra in your gut.

Step 6: Bring the mantra into the second chakra, the sacral, and feel the emotion of the mantra (joy/gratitude/power).

Step 7: Bring the mantra into the first chakra, the root base of the spine, and feel you already have it.

Step 8: Bring the mantra down to the earth chakra, below your feet, and root it down into the center of the Earth to manifest it.

Healing the Inner Child Emotional Wounds: Re-Parenting

There are many ways to work with your inner child. You can use a photograph from childhood or a doll (male or female) that represents you at a young age. Every inner child has a joyful, magical, wondrous side. The wounded side is where healing is needed for the magic of the inner child to return.

Personally, I have found the deepest way to heal the inner child is to travel inward and see, feel, and observe childhood experiences that created the wound. Some experiences seem insignificant, while others are traumatic. All experiences play a role.

The wounded inner child is still living as a wounded child but is now an adult. The energy of hurtful circumstances has lingered somewhere in the human energy field, causing disharmony in areas of your life. The mind remembers the hardships and feelings that were cultivated long ago and is still living by those experiences. The pain of being bullied, feeling insecure or rejected, abandoned, not smart enough, and not fitting in is still living within, causing discord and blocking abundance. This is your baggage to be transformed. Being an adult does not indicate you are healed or that you have overcome the hurtful experiences of your childhood. In fact, more likely, you have successfully suppressed those energies as they contribute to behaviors, actions, and the decisions in adult life that usually create more disharmony and hurt. These wounds block love, joy, success, freedom, and the true power of creativity.

Your inner child wants to grow up. It does not want to hold onto the pain of childhood, adolescence or adulthood. It deeply desires to be whole, to feel the love of self, others, and God. This sacred, precious part of you was formed by the external world and wants desperately to let go of the past to live an abundant life. Ultimately, your inner child wants to be unconditionally loved by you.

Most people are willing to look at the mind, its beliefs and thoughts, especially if changing a thought helps us get what we want. But what about our emotions and life traumas? Too often this extraordinary part of us has not been developed well. We love to feel love and joy, but we don't like to feel pain, anger, or hurt.

Emotions are little blessings from God. These beautiful energies make us human. Without them we would be like robots and devoid of feeling and expression. As we grew into adulthood, we learned how to suppress our emotions and hide our vulnerable sides. Many of us were taught that to be a big girl or boy was to refrain from expressing emotions, in particular anger, disappointment, and sadness. Why does growing up indicate the need to stop being an emotional, feeling human being? It doesn't. If you have difficulty expressing how you feel as an adult, it might be because you were taught to shut down your feelings at an early age.

Honoring all your emotions is a very important piece of healing inner-child wounds. Opening your emotional flow and working with it in a healing capacity is very empowering and liberating! As an adult you must be able to manage, handle, and work with your emotions without projecting them on others. You know the range of emotions and feelings you have in a day. When they are not honored and released, they get stuck in the emotional body, which directly affects your physical health as well as your ability to give and receive love. Feelings can range from angry to happy, sad to joy, lonely to loved, disappointed to contented, frustrated to accepting, anxious to calm, hysterical to rational, and so on. Feeling like a victim, inadequate, unloved, insecure, or stupid are all ways in which wounds remain intact. Begin paying attention to your emotions and feelings. Write them down in a journal even if they don't make logical sense. Gently allow them to surface with the intention to transform them. As I like to say: Grieve them, don't feed them! Behind the grief is your true empowerment.

An overloaded emotional body is one of the first causes of disease. Emotions must be able to flow through the human energy field and not get stuck somewhere along the way, such as in the liver or heart. As lower emotions are purged, love, joy, peace, and freedom emerge naturally as the Soul steps forward.

Subsequently, I was shown how important it is to understand my emotions (emotional body). Being courageous enough to feel them as they are purged from every cell in the mind and body creates a shift in energy that allows transformation. The physical body receives great benefits from releasing dense emotional energy as it gains a greater sense of physical well-being, mental clarity, and balanced emotions. Imagine releasing twenty pounds of emotional weight repeatedly until all lifetimes are healed? Our human bodies would be free of disease and appear as a translucent being of love and light. That is evolution!

Human Thought Field

I was trained as a Thought Field therapist, which gave me the ability to see the connection between thoughts, feelings, and emotions. The human thought field is a massive field of energy containing thoughts, emotions, and feelings that are all interconnected. One thought leads to a feeling which leads to an emotion. One feeling leads to an emotion which leads to a thought. The process continues around a cycle of thoughts, feelings, and emotions, creating discord until that layer is released and healed. In our human lives we have experienced many thousands of layers of thought fields that represent our current levels of consciousness. Therein, we must heal the negative layers of thought fields, untrue beliefs, and negative emotions that suppress the greatness of the Soul. Once we understand how our own thought fields are intersected, we will see how interconnected we are to the matrix of all Souls.

After receiving certification in this modality, my mind automatically began piecing together the fragments of my wounds when in meditation. I decided it was necessary to go deeper into my subconscious.

One day bright yellow rays of the sun shone through the kitchen window, sprinkling a hue of rainbow colors on the wall. Spirit guides whispered into my ear, "Go into your healing room."

The little blue healing room offered soothing feelings of inner peace. Two double windows on the left revealed the emergence of spring. Green grass and colorful flowers newly sprouted from the ground were beauty to the senses. I felt calm. I sat in a dark blue swivel chair, lit a candle, and placed crystals on the healing table directly in front of me.

> *Taking a few deep breaths, I closed my eyes, inviting in my spirit guides. Instantly my mind spiraled into my inner world, and I am thrust back in time as a young child of about age eight.*
>
> *"Share your toy with your sister, Pauline," says Mom.*
>
> *"I don't want to share. This is my toy. She has more than I do."*
>
> *"You're being selfish," Mom says in a demanding tone.*
>
> *I feel a block to go deeper at this point. Emotions are surfacing, and I realize something is blocking them. A battle between the wounded ego and Soul exists. The Soul wants the circumstance purged from my energy field, while the ego is terrified to feel what might emerge from going deeper.*
>
> *I'm frustrated by the blockage and wonder, How can I get to the root of this?*
>
> *Master guide speaks, "Pauline, you are no different than anyone else. The wounds you have experienced and feel are the same as every human being. You are not alone, dear one."*
>
> *Tears stream down my face.*
>
> *Thank God I am not alone in this. Thank God everyone else feels the same way.*

I believed I was the only person who felt hurt and inadequate. Now realizing everyone has the same baggage in one form or another, I am relieved to go deeper into the wounded ego.

My mind revisits the scene.

I don't reply to my mom and feel angered that I am being forced to share my toy. Perfection is expected of me, and I don't want the role. Why can't I just be a child? I remain stubborn. I feel invalidated. I stand my ground as my toy remains clutched in my arms.

"I wouldn't want to be your friend because you don't share," Mom says firmly.

A pain in my heart triggers feelings of unworthiness. I am a bad person because I don't want to share my toy.

I feel sorry for the little girl. I cry for the eight-year-old child who felt misunderstood and invalidated. Mom didn't understand why I didn't want to share; nor could I explain my true feelings. The direct statement that I wasn't worthy of having a good friend embedded itself in the emotional body long ago, and now it was surfacing. I cry in deep heaves, just like a child.

The scene changes.

I see myself in grammar school. The teacher creates a height and weight chart. I am the heaviest child in the class.

Feelings and thoughts of being humiliated by being overweight run through my body as I remember hating that weight chart. Why did the teacher want to humiliate me? I don't fit in with the other kids.

Looking at the younger self, I understand what is needed. In that moment I decide to be my own mother and speak with the eight-year-old.

Pauline, it's me. I love you and understand how you feel. It's okay you didn't want to share your toy. You are worthy of being loved and having true friends. You don't need to stuff down your emotions any longer. I am here to help you purge everything that has ever hurt you. Being a bit overweight was a protection; you don't need to protect yourself anymore.

I am sobbing deeply for the inner child.

The scene changes.

The eight-year-old Pauline grows up to about ten years of age.

She is wearing a beautiful Easter outfit of navy blue and yellow and a matching Easter bonnet. She stands with perfect posture, looks pretty, and is smiling. I sense how sensitive she is, now realizing she's empathic. The young girl wonders, Am I pretty enough, am I loved? All I want is love.

The scene changes to a conversation with my father.

You're just too sensitive, Pauline. You need to grow a thicker skin." Tears stream down my face. I feel so misguided. No one understands me. The world doesn't make sense. I don't want to be here.

Now I remember how and why I grew a thick skin, and gained weight to protect myself, developing a superior façade of confidence by attaining material possessions, a pattern of my father. Mom accumulated material possessions to fill the lack from her childhood. I feel dislike for myself.

Seeing how my inner child was trying to be so perfect to gain love, I lovingly tell her,

Relax, Pauline. You don't have anything to prove to anyone, nor do you need to protect yourself. You're perfect just as you are. Your sensitivities are a gift. Nor do you need material possessions to feel confident. I love you, I love you, I love you. Learn to love yourself more. Everyone is equal.

Returning into my body from this experience, my eyes were opened to glance around the healing space. The room seemed illuminated. I felt like I was floating in a bubble of love and peace; it was surreal. At first I was confused by what had just happened. Then I realized many layers of my thought field had opened, and I was able to go back in time to heal my inner child.

Great compassion for this child was felt as I began to nurture her in ways my biological parents didn't. No blame existed as I acknowledged the responsibility to heal my life was completely mine and only mine. My parents did the best they could, and they were very good parents. Spiritual work moves beyond blame and recognizes the beauty of growth that occurs in all circumstances. The Sweet, Sour, Salty worksheet was being revealed.

The World Mirror

> Every relationship you have is a reflection of the
> relationship you are having with yourself. (Gabriel)

Everything we see in the world that is perceived to be good, bad, right, or wrong is a mirror. Yes, everything! When a wounded ego trait in another person or situation triggers a visceral reaction within you, it is because you have seen a reflection of yourself in some way. Family, friends (especially a spouse), teachers, politicians, religious leaders, world events, poverty, animal cruelty are all mirrors in which to see every aspect within humankind that needs to be transformed. We see different traits depending on the traits we need to work on. Without a mirror we cannot see the parts of us that need transformation; nor can greatness be recognized. The mirror initially reflects a visceral reaction to traits that are lower in vibration before higher vibrational traits are acknowledged, such as unconditional love, compassion, unity, peace, and so on.

The world and everyone it in became my mirror. Every time I was triggered—by what someone said, did, or didn't do, or acted in a way I disapproved of, or by an event in the world—I recognized it represented a mirror into the wounded parts of me. Perhaps I contributed to a dysfunctional world through my own wounding. What would happen if I contributed more love and compassion through my own healing and awakening? We are not separate from the collective consciousness. We are a part of it, creating positive or negative outcomes for ourselves and the world. Do you believe the world can evolve into something better? Or do you maintain a mindset that history only repeats itself?

What patterns do you see in the world? Do you see selfishness, arrogance, neediness, insecurity, manipulation, ignorance, and hate? Do you see loneliness, fear, anger, control, superiority, inferiority, greed, corruption, abuse, the need to be right, or the need to win?

If you perceive that someone is lonely, longing for more love, and you feel the pain of their loneliness, then you probably have the same pattern, loneliness.

If you meet someone who is sloppy, and the sloppiness triggers you, then you are probably sloppy in some way. There are many ways to be sloppy. The specific way that one person is sloppy is not necessarily the same way another person is sloppy. Perhaps you perceive the person as sloppy because you have seen the individual's atrocious eating habits. But your sloppiness could be in the way you don't clean your house or the way you are disorganized in business. If you are absolutely not sloppy in any area of your life (which I highly doubt) then you must be a "neat freak," and some part of you would like to be a little sloppier in a healthy way. You might be too hard on yourself, and your neatness keeps you in a structured pattern that limits you from living more openly. You may deeply desire to break free from being so rigid, and so the sloppiness annoys you.

When you see an example of forgiveness and love in another, you may be triggered because you, too, want to be able to forgive and love in the same way. Is there not some part of you that longs to be able to forgive totally?

We see greatness every day exhibited by those who are courageous enough to take a stand and go against the grain of society for the good of all people. There are people who have been acknowledged as great leaders and they, too, reflect our own greatness. But are you courageous enough to step into your greatness?

Every time you comment on another's behavior in a negative way, you are looking in the mirror. Every time you comment on another's behavior in a positive way, you have the ability to become that way too! If you already possess those beautiful qualities, you'll be uplifted, not triggered. We see the greatness in others so easily, but can you see the greatness within yourself? As the ego is transformed, your God-given greatness emerges through the awakening of the Soul.

Once I was speaking on the phone with a friend while she complained about her boyfriend. As she described his actions, I blurted out, "He's arrogant." I felt a twinge in my body, knowing this trigger reflected something within me. I headed into the little blue room immediately after hanging up the phone.

> *With eyes closed, I asked spirit and my Soul to join this healing. I took a few deep breaths and instantly fell deep into the inner world of the wounded ego.*
>
> *I questioned, why was I triggered by his arrogance?*
>
> *Spirit speaks, "You are not arrogant; you are insecure. At least he has some degree of power. He speaks his mind while you do not."*
>
> *Tears roll down my face. It's true, I can't speak up. I'm afraid to voice my opinion because what if I say something the other person won't like? Will they still like or love me?*

My mind shifts from hearing to seeing another scene from childhood.

> *Mom was scolding me for something. I tried to defend myself by explaining my side of the story, but all I hear is Mom saying, "Don't answer me back." My emotions and voice were stifled.*
>
> *Spirit speaks, "Learn to speak up without being in defense. Build the confidence to speak up."*

On returning, I declared my right to speak up and be heard. Continued healing sessions kept digging deeper into my subconscious, churning up thoughts and feelings I was unaware existed. Again I was filled with lightness and slight fatigue. And miraculously, the trigger was gone. I lay down to rest.

Don't worry that you have ego insecurities and weaknesses;

everyone has them. Laugh about them, but do address them with love and acceptance. Those traits will dissolve easily, and you'll begin to feel freedom of the Soul.

How Do Others Experience You?

> Whenever you are about to find fault with someone, ask yourself the following question: What fault of mine most nearly resembles the one I am about to criticize? (Marcus Aurelius)

It's simple to observe how others behave and how their behavior makes you feel. You know how it feels to be rejected, hurt, annoyed, betrayed, gossiped about, abandoned, disrespected, and unheard and unseen by people around you. Looking on the flip side, how do you think others feel when you engage in the same behaviors? Do you think they find you annoying? Selfish? Self-absorbed? Disrespectful? Domineering? Gossipy? Complaining? Negative? Manipulative? Try to imagine what it might feel like to be another person who is in your company. It is unrealistic to think that others behave badly while you do not.

As my inner worlds were being revealed, the wounds and hereditary patterns of the wounded ego, I began to think about everything I was learning about myself. Again the veil lifted, and I was given the ability to "see" into the wounds quite clearly, not only for myself, but for others for the purposes of healing. Then I thought, *Oh goodness! How do others experience me?* Talk about being humbled by the insights of the Soul!

Grabbing the Sweet, Sour, Salty worksheet for review, I thought, *This is going to take a lifetime to heal. Oh no. Not one but many, many lifetimes to heal!* I burst into laughter. The process was fascinating. Never before had I been so enchanted by anything like the unfolding of myself, the discovery of me, the awakening of my Soul.

With the new awareness, I decided to be honest at first try. With pencil and paper in hand, I scanned the genetics worksheet. Several words popped out like a jack-in-the-box, and I wrote them down. Honestly looking at myself from my husband's perspective, I discovered he probably felt controlled and bossed around. These traits were indeed playing a role in our relationship. He also probably saw me as being very competent, a good cook, and smart. These parts needed no attention as they were stable and beneficial. Yet the controlling, bossy parts really needed transformation. New traits I wished to replace the old ones with were, being more agreeable, accepting, and less judgmental.

This is a lifetime of inner work, and well worth the honesty.

Tracey

Tracey was an amazing woman to work with. She was organized, educated, and willing to look at herself with little effort. I felt respect for her immediately. She admitted wounded ego traits in the very first session. It usually takes a few sessions before a person begins opening up, divulging their deep, dark secrets. She spoke openly about the issues in her life without reservation. Her energy was strong, confident, and structured.

Her biggest problem was with her eldest son. In her view, he was lazy and did not apply himself to anything. He was irresponsible and had no direction in his life. This caused Tracey to feel frustrated, and she worried about his future. She would often say that she knew her boy was intelligent with a drive to succeed, but she could not bring it out in him. The more she lectured him on how he needed to get his act together, the more he withdrew.

Intuitively, I knew she was correct about her boy but that she was going about it the wrong way. He was not responding to structure and being told what to do. I asked her, "How do you think Brian experiences you?"

She looked at me with a blank stare for a few moments and then answered, "I don't know."

"Yes you do. Think about it for a few minutes, and just let yourself speak any words that come to mind."

After few moments of silence, she said, "Controlling, too strong, hard on him."

I then asked her to think about how it might feel if someone were controlling her or came on too strong toward her. She admitted that it would not feel good at all. So I suggested that perhaps it would not feel good to Brian either. Instantly she saw the bigger picture and accepted it without resistance. Brian was not having a good experience with his mom, and she needed to change how she addressed him. My intuitive sense was that all he wanted was to be shown love and to feel accepted by his parents, especially his father. Dad was asked to take a larger role in Brian's life.

Tracey and I worked on her being softer and more loving. We talked about not giving him directions or orders but speaking in a nonjudgmental way about the things that he felt inspired by. One of the most powerful moments in Tracey's growth was when I suggested that she simply hold a space for Brian to be the best person he could be. Not for him to be the person she wanted him to be, but for Brian to be the best man that would make him happy within himself. Amazingly Tracey and her husband were able to follow the suggestions.

Within a short time, her son's attitude changed. He went back to school and became more responsible. Not only was the relationship with her child improving, she started to like herself a little more too!

Holding Space

If you see someone struggling and not able to speak about how he or she feels, you can help that person by holding space for the individual to rise above the trauma. Not everyone is open and feels safe to express pain. You can hold a space for them to embody strength, or self-love, or confidence, or whatever they need to assist them without trying to jump in to save them. Trying to save someone often backfires with resentment from both parties. Holding space for them to find their own answers and God-given strengths will empower them. To hold spaces for others, simply visualize them as being the best versions of themselves without the need to control the outcome. This does not require talking or directing. The only requirement is to maintain a vision of that person rising above his or her limitations. Perhaps when the moment presents itself, a word or two reinforcing positive actions, as well as encouragement to overcome limitations, is appropriate.

We feel the energy of thoughts and feelings that others have toward us. If someone feels we are stupid, we will feel the energy of the word without hearing it. As a result, it becomes part of our subconscious mind. Then we may begin to act out the imposed feeling or thought. We must hold visions of each other in the truth of an empowered Soul, even when someone has acted less than that. Acting less than the greatness of the Soul is only an indication of trauma or insecurity. Trust that every person has an empowered Soul, and to the best of your ability, see them as that.

Facing the Fears

As Lou once said, "Conquer your fears, and you will know who you are." We humans have many fears living within the conscious and subconscious mind. It's just part of living in the human condition.

How do you conquer fears?

You dive right into them! Fear them not as they are not the true you! The courage to dive into them, knowing they simply need your love and attention, is inherent and comes from the Soul. Once you accept that fears are only wounded parts of the fragile ego, they will dissolve more easily.

It occurred to me that fear is our deepest enemy, yet it is purely an illusion. The Soul doesn't embrace fear; only a wounded ego does. I began to see some of the fears that had been holding me back in life. I asked my spirit guides to help release them through transformation into confidence.

Spirit guided me to the internet, where I found a wonderful book on fears. According to the authors there are four basic fears: fear of success, fear of failure, fear of rejection, and fear of abandonment. As I read this book, deeper triggers pinged inside my body.

Through my perception, these four fears are at the root of every other fear we have, and there are many. Some fears are conscious, but most are subconscious. The subconscious fears are the most complicated because they are hidden. Operating unknowingly, these fears create stumbling blocks and obstacles in life, creating one challenge after another toward achieving a goal or dream come true. The saboteur and victim part of the ego works subtly behind the scenes, justifying why you are unworthy to create what you desire, or falsely justifying why it won't work out.

There is a simple way to deal with fears. Follow the emotional and mental longing of the desire. Don't judge the insights as good or bad. Assume to some degree you've got every fear preventing the manifestation of your desire. To deny the existence of your deepest fears is to deny your Soul's love and power. Many layers of fear exist that keep you from knowing who you are on the Soul level and creating a life filled with miracles.

For every desire there is a fear of having what you want and not having what you want. There are many sides to fear. You might want to feel more power and confidence, more love, freedom, prosperity, or creativity. Healing your life may be a deep desire. If you have tried to create these desires without success, it may be because you have not addressed the fear elements of having it and not having it.

As fears are released, the heart will need to be open to receive that which you have asked for. God is willing to provide you with abundance in all areas of life since that is the original pattern of creation.

Every item on the Sweet, Sour, Salty worksheet was related to fear in some way. As I delved into my dark side, my innermost fears began to sprout up like weeds in fertile soil. Once I embraced each fear with love and acceptance, the life-force energy of the weeds wilted and lost their hold on me. Without the deep-seated fears of the ego, I could embrace my Soul's love and true power. I could finally expand authentically. Ego fears are insignificant and miniscule compared to the fears of knowing your Soul. It's much easier to remain small and insignificant than it is to rise up and become the magnificent being that God created you to be.

Living in limitation and fear is commonplace. What's uncertain and frightening to the ego is the true power of greatness, love, compassion, unity, joy, and freedom. At the Soul level, these qualities are foreign to us as a collective until the awakening.

Example 1: Desire and Longing for More Love

- I observed the deeper fears of having love and the fears of not having love as they connect to fear of abandonment and rejection.
- I delved into the deeper emotions and thoughts. What fears existed within regarding love?
- The fear of having love created fears of being vulnerable, fear of loss, rejection, and abandonment, fear of receiving and then abusing that love, taking it for granted, fear of being hurt and betrayed.
- The fear of not having love created fear of being alone, fear of not being loveable, fear of not being worthy of being loved, fear of not being able to receive, fear of not being cared for.

Example 2: Desire for Money, Wealth, and Security

- I observed the fears of having money and the fears of not having money as they connect to the fears of success and failure.
- I delved into the deeper emotions and thoughts. What fears existed within regarding money?
- The fear of being wealthy created fears of having too much while others have so little.
- The fear of feeling guilty creeped into being wealthy, along with the possibility of becoming greedy and corrupt. There was fear of using wealth unwisely and wasting it on material things, rather than being responsible with it. Fear of success and power was the ultimate fear of being wealthy.
- The fear of not being wealthy created fears of being poor, of not having enough, of starving, and survival. This fear created more lack and poverty patterns. Fear of failure existed, so why bother trying was at the root cause.

Example 3: Desire to be Healthy

- I observed the fears of being healthy, and the fears of not being healthy as they connect to success, failure, rejection, or abandonment.
- I delved into the deeper emotions and thoughts. What fears existed within regarding health?
- The fear of being healthy didn't exist unless there was a health issue to begin with, which brought a secondary gain, such as attention, caretaking, and fear of releasing codependence. Fear of being independent, and capable of taking care of one's own needs.
- Fears of being unhealthy were fear of being sick, unable to live well, not having control over the Self, being a victim of life, fear of death.

Any institution or person who has placed fear on you with respect to creating your own health, prosperity, wellness, love, or feeling worthy, has taken away your power. It's time to take your power back. Working through the deeper fears in this way will result in an awakening of the Soul, exuding strength, courage, and true power to create an abundant life. As fears, emotions, and thoughts are transformed, wholeness from within develops. A true sense of self grows in communion with God. In this way we maintain control over ourselves, not others, nor can others control us.

If someone hurts you, takes his or her love away, or passes away, we will be jolted at first. But forgiveness, understanding, and healing soon follow as your own sense of self-love remembers who you are—a being of love and light whose source is God.

Releasing to the Full Moon

What is it about a full moon that sparks intrigue? When the moon glows like a beautiful white ball of light in the midnight sky, we can't help but feel in awe of it. With its majestic qualities, we are lured into its energy and captivated by something mystical. Centuries ago, witches and healers sought curative energy on a monthly basis as the full moon never failed to appear and offer its healing powers. Luna in her fullness represents feminine powers of illumination, revealing what is hidden.

When the moon is full, a blue rim forms around it. This is when its power is heightened, and the opportunity to connect with the divine feminine and release fears and unwanted blockages is present. Each month I began the practice of connecting with the mysterious ball of white light to release what no longer served me.

I asked the moon goddess to heal a few areas of my life, releasing fears or insecurities. Sometimes I was very specific in my healing request and directly asked the moon to help me surrender my fears about writing this book. And, of course, I asked the moon to help me surrender the reasons why I wanted a child, and if a child were not part of my path, then to accept it, move on, and trust that the path of service to God was enough for me.

I would often ask the divine feminine or Blessed Mother to help me release control over my ego as it pertained to my husband. I did not want to control him on any level and realized I was doing so. Another request was to help me release control over my life and my spiritual path. I let go of the need to conform to a mainstream life, so I could love myself as the Soul God created me to be, or who the world thought I should be. I knew that if I were to reach my Soul's true destiny, I would have to let go of trying to control it.

One winter evening I stared at a beautiful full moon shining into my living room. The room was dark as no lights were turned on. Yet Luna illuminated the room from a cloudless night sky filled with twinkling stars. The cosmos was beautiful and mysterious, yet friendly and supportive. Gazing into the moon's glow, I was pulled into its magnetic field. A blue rim appeared. I stared hard. Breathing gently in and out as the moon's grasp had a hold on me, I was swept gently away into surrender, releasing control patterns.

I felt energy pulsating through my body as dense negative energy was broken up to be released. Healing was occurring. Not until the energy stopped flowing could I ask for healing in another area.

The exercise is very easy. Simply gaze upon a full moon with an unobstructed view. Breathe deeply in and out, and then close your eyes. Set your intention to connect with the healing power of the divine feminine. Invite in your spirit guides, the angels, and ask them to assist you. Open your eyes and stare at the moon. Continue staring at it until you see the blue rim. Not everyone can see it, so don't worry if you cannot. Trust that your desire to heal using this method is valid and will be acknowledged by the divine. As you continue to stare at the moon, state the reason for your healing.

Stay with your intention, and do not look away from the moon. Let feelings or thoughts surface until you feel a shift. Once you feel a shift, your work is completed. If you don't feel a shift, don't worry.

That which is unseen and unfelt is still occurring. I would advise that you work with the energy of the moon no longer than five to ten minutes. It's that powerful!

In my overzealousness to evolve, on one occasion I released far too much in one evening. Looking at the moon, I was swept away with each request for healing. This is not a good idea! I don't suggest releasing to the moon everything that you want to be free of in one night! While immediately afterwards I felt light, buoyant, full of love, and joyous beyond belief, the next morning and several days afterwards I was barely able to function physically. So go slowly! My body was very sore and stiff and felt like it had been hit by a truck, not to mention the exhaustion.

When the moon is new, ask for new things to come into your life. With each new moon I asked the divine feminine to help me awaken to my Soul. I asked for courage, love, divine guidance, and protection. As I asked for more love, I received my cat kids—all six of them!

It was interesting that during my seven years of graceful isolation, I never asked for anything material. Since the focus of spiritual work is about healing and evolution, the material world did not appeal to me at this time because my material needs were met. If your material needs aren't met and something material is needed, then ask for it.

I trusted that as I awakened and followed the path of God, the material world, my prosperity, and my ability to pay my bills each month would take care of itself. And indeed it was taken care of.

Sometimes Lou would join in the purge ritual. We'd have fun with it. It is a wonderful way to connect privately with the energy of Creator to receive healing and guidance.

If for some reason the sky is clouded and the full moon is hidden, you can still engage in this exercise. You will need unwavering trust in your ability to connect with that which isn't visible yet exists. The new moon is not visible either, so here is an excellent exercise in setting your intention and learning to trust the unseen metaphysical world.

Each time you heal an aspect of your life, you are retrieving a part of your Soul that has been suppressed through trauma. Your Soul is always with you, but if it is suppressed by life circumstances, it can't function to serve you through the wounds of the ego. The wounds must be healed, and as this is done, the Soul awakens more strongly to guide you. Soul retrieval through all lifetimes is possible and necessary to become an empowered, sovereign being.

Every person is responsible for his or her own transformation. We must hold visions of a peaceful, abundant world, not through force, but through transformation and evolution. One of the most difficult yet exciting steps to heal your life and awaken your Soul is to use the mirror exercises. To recognize aspects about yourself that need your love and attention is very liberating. It takes a lot of energy to pretend to be something that you are not. It takes a lot of energy to stuff down emotions that you do not want to feel, and it takes a lot of energy to keep up with belief systems that do not work. Letting go is true freedom.

As my life healed, it seemed this might be the best time to start a family. I had a plan. Two children would grow up with love, understanding of their Soul and connection to God, holistic living and eating, no vaccinations, herbal medicine, meditation, and homeschooling if necessary. The vision was perfect.

Conclusion: With all my flaws, insecurities, imperfections, and mistakes, I am still lovable and worthy. Becoming empowered is about exploring all the ways in which you must love yourself. It has nothing to do with anyone else. In the wake of your wounds lies your greatness.

CHAPTER 7

THE GREAT SURRENDER

Trust in the lord with all thine heart; and lean
not unto thine own understanding. In all thy ways
acknowledge Him, and He shall direct thy paths.

Proverbs 3:5–6 (KJV)

Each of us has a unique path. Do not try to walk the path of another for it will not bring satisfaction. Do not use the voice of another for it has already been spoken. Do not try to look like another for you do yourself an injustice.

Be unique. Be different. Be bold. Do this because you love who you are!

God does not interfere with our choices. We are given the choice to follow divine will or ego will. This is the power and control we have over our lives. God gives us free will of the ego, but is it a good thing? The choice to follow ego will is stronger than the surrender to follow God's will because we have not been taught how to co-create with

God through surrender. We are masters of creating what we think we want to fulfill in our lives through the ego mind.

Transforming the wounded ego, the inner walls to awaken my truth continued to crumble. New questions popped into my awareness. *What kind of life am I creating through my ego, and what kind of life could I co-create with God? What life did I need to lose in order to find an authentic one? Who am I, and why am I here?*

Releasing the need to conform to my family or a traditional life in general started a process of surrender. A little rebel within was peeking its head out from under the stifling ways of Earth life. I was learning to surrender to the will of God rather than to live by the will of my ego or what I perceived to be a fulfilling life.

The Great Surrender

New house, new baby, right? It had been nearly a year, and my body would not succumb to pregnancy. Despite healthy living, a deep desire to create children, all the healing work I had been doing, the perfect home and plan for a family, manifestation did not occur. I felt confused, hurt, and angry. Mothering came easy to me as a natural-born nurturer. Everyone said I'd be the perfect mom. Intuitively, I knew this to be true. Every psychic reading foretold of children. In denial and attempting to control my fate, I stressed on to create what I believed my Soul desired. Years ago my spirit guide spoke vaguely about children in my life. What exactly did her words mean? I was about to find out.

Determined to understand why my body refused conception, I delved deep inside my subconscious, setting an intention to release the pain and confusion of not conceiving a child.

An invocation to begin all healing sessions blurted out of my mouth, "I am grounded and protected, asking only those of the highest nature in spirit guides, angels, and ascended masters to assist in the healing of this issue."

Several crystals are placed on the massage table in front of me and two candles are lit on the desk behind. Sitting quietly in the little blue room for a few minutes with eyes closed, I focus on my heart. Thoughts immediately surface from deep within my subconscious about the pain of not having a child. My mind became very active as I slip into the inner world of my shadow.

Why me? Why not me? What's wrong with me, am I not good enough? Life is not fair? I'm confused. Life sucks. Why can't I have a child? I would be an amazing mother. Why do I even want a child? Nothing makes sense!

I feel emotional, alone, unloved, and empty despite prior healing sessions, when love and connection to God filled my being.

I start to cry and grieve that I did not have a child. A new feeling swept over me as I became entranced. Something had taken me over to which I had no control. Deeper tears surface, touching the pain body. My heart hurt physically and emotionally. I grieve for myself, my life, for everyone who has struggled in this way. I feel sad and lonely, like a victim, all alone in a world I do not understand at all.

No one loves me. How will I be happy without a child?

I feel humiliated, insignificant, and stupid with the realization that these feelings govern some part of me. The energy begins to subside, and my eyes remain closed as the next layer of emotion bubbles up.

The scene shifts.

> *I feel fearful of becoming a light worker and for my future as a healer. Could walking this path fall out from under me at any moment? My body shudders at the thought. Tears keep flowing. Fear of an uncertain future races through my body. Who am I? What kind of life am I living? A woman who lives the life of a light worker? I am so odd. Why is my life so distorted? I'm afraid. Who will believe me? Who will love me? Will I be laughed at, accepted, or rejected? My body trembles in fear and self-rejection. I hate myself. I am disgusting and worthless.*
>
> *Tears continue to stream from swollen eyes and down red cheeks. Again, the energy begins to subside. But then with eyes still closed, I feel the next wave of emotion pushing up from deep within. I am on a roller coaster ride of emotions.*

The scene shifts.

> *I feel hatred for the world. I hate the war in Iraq and those responsible for creating it. Why, God, why? I remember all the people and soldiers who were killed. My heart pounds with pain as I envision the World Trade Center burning, collapsing, and killing so many innocent workers, bystanders, firefighters, and police officers. Unbearable pain fills my heart, and I feel like I am dying. God, what kind of world do I live in? I'm so sad and grief-stricken for the loss of so many lives. The pain of everyone on the planet is inside me. Hatred, all the hate that is living inside every person on Earth is inside me. My*

God, this hatred is enormous, and it's living inside me, and everyone else!

My body reacts autonomously. I am bawling like a child, stomping my feet in anger. I don't want hate or pain inside me! This is not who I am! Palpitations and a burning sensation are releasing from my heart and then travel up my chest, throat, and out of my mouth. I cough uncontrollably and spew out the negative energy that inhabits my beautiful heart. I cry with passion and scream out ugliness and anger. Physically, it is painful to release. God, why do people do what they do!

Tears continue to flow like a river. I am exhausted and tired, but darkness is lifting. A few moments later, my heart feels clear and wide open.

The scene shifts.

I see myself growing up as a teenager into adulthood, always seeking to fill the love that was missing in my life. I cry even harder for this person who could not find enough love. I feel loveless and unworthy of being loved. Anger at those who did not understand me or who attempted to control me purged from my energy field. I cry for the adult who had been hurt and betrayed, who had been divorced twice, and who feels rejected and abandoned.

Slowly returning from my trance, the tears stopped, and my body calmed. Massive amounts of darkness were purged. Somehow I ended up on the floor while trying to make some kind of logical sense out of what just occurred, but I could not. There was no rational explanation; it just happened. Setting the intention to heal the pain of not conceiving opened up another layer of emotional baggage needing to be released, yet it was completely unrelated. The human thought-field is massive. All issues are interconnected in some way. I had no idea the degree to which I would be swept away into the subconscious. Once the purge started, I had no control over it until it was finished. It lasted about an hour and a half.

Unintentionally, I tuned into mass consciousness or the collective mind. The mind, body, and Soul are one energy system connected to every other mind, body, and Soul on the planet. I see this connection as a matrix of all Souls. These are the thoughts and feelings of every person on Earth to some degree, including myself, which was an astounding insight. Who knew we were so intricately connected? But we are.

True healing runs deep and dark to crack open the wounds for the light to enter. Nothing seemed dark now. Everything appeared light and bright and unusually translucent. The furniture, the rug, the windows, and the paintings on the wall seemed to lose their solidity. With wobbly legs I managed to hoist myself up, holding onto the massage table. Hobbling to the window I looked outside to view the grass, garden, shrubs, and trees. All seemed to have an iridescent glow about them. The sky was clear blue, and in that moment, I felt the love of God in my heart, mind, and body once again. Unconditional love and gratitude emerged, bringing inner peace. With each entranced purge the healings went deeper, leaving me with feelings of freedom, love, and joy. The depth of emotion and feelings was extraordinary, like nothing I've ever felt before.

Being swept away like that was profound and scary, yet freeing and exhilarating! Wanting to experience this again, I began purging daily, sometimes twice a day. This became the pattern of my life for seven years of graceful isolation. One of the greatest gifts I had ever been given. Through these experiences I learned about who I am and began to embody the energy of the divine. My body and metabolism changed. It seemed the aging process began to reverse itself, and I became healthier in mind, body, and Soul.

Sometimes purging was instantaneous and erupted without

warning. Soon I developed the skill to purge massive amounts of energy quickly. Peace, love, joy, and beauty then filled my mind and body. In the little blue healing room I was being shown the way into the Soul. *Who in God's name am I?*

Inner thoughts connected to a massive human thought-field led into the myriad emotions living within me connected to unfulfilled yearnings. Yes, all unfulfilled desires show up as a desire for something outside the self, yet the only true yearning is internal—to awaken the Soul and reconnect with God. As soon as I acknowledged undesirable ego thoughts, my emotional body burst open with feelings and emotions connected to the pain of not conceiving, as well as feelings having nothing to do with a child at all.

I was healing myself of the deeper, more unconscious reasons of why I wanted a child. An insight came to me afterwards. Do we desire to have children because we seek to heal our own inner child? Do we have children to live through them? To heal through them? Do we have children because we believe they will bring us the ultimate happiness and fulfillment? Do we have children because we think that is what we are supposed to do or feel obligated to do? Do we have children to learn about unconditional love? Is it selfish not to procreate? Many insights came through this experience.

Battle of the Wills

Unknowingly I had not yet surrendered completely to my Soul's path. We must continue to choose this path and do the inner work, or we will be pulled back into what the ego believes is best. The ego continues to protect itself with false thoughts about what would fulfill itself. Many layers of beliefs and wounds run deep to maintain the status quo.

Still forcing my ego will, I had an idea. If my body wouldn't conceive, surely adoption was the answer. Papers to adopt a child came swiftly from the INS. Profiles of many beautiful children waiting to be loved by a mom and dad arrived from the adoption agency. At this time, adoptions from Russia and Romania were common. Young male and female children ranging in age from six months to sixteen years hoped for loving homes. I had everything to offer these children, including the love they deserved. Loving them as I would a child from my own body would be easy. It never occurred to me that a child born to another person wouldn't be my child to love, nurture, and provide the guidance to live fully. Two children would be perfect. When the divine heart is open to love, there is no boundary as to whom or how that love is given. We are one Soul, one love.

Adoption papers were strewn on the dining room table. Cautiously examining the information requirements, I filled out section one, including our name, address, income, and education. A chill ran down the back of my spine.

The voice spoke to my mind, *"This is not the path I have in mind for you."*

Jolted by hearing this message, I sat back in the chair and felt confused. I spoke aloud, "What do you mean this is not the path you have in mind for me? Am I not following everything you wish of me? Am I not being prepared to be a mother, to love a child as if coming from my body? Is this not the test, dear God? Am I not meant to bring awareness of unity and love to the world?"

All was quiet. The voice did not speak again. I returned to filling out the paperwork. Then, I felt a twinge in my stomach and burst into tears.

"Oh God, you speak the damn truth!" I yelled out. "You have guided me for many years never to fail, never to misguide, never to hurt. Yet I am hurting by this truth." I wiped my eyes with my hands.

"Why am I not being given the gift of a child? I am the perfect mother! Have you not filled my heart with love for this very reason?" I bellowed. Waiting several minutes for a response, only silence remained.

"If I am not to be their mother, then who will be? Who will love them as I can? Who?" I shouted out.

In that moment I was challenged with following the free will of my ego or the will of God. The choice was mine, and I had full control. Ego will resembles conformity, the status quo, desires of earthly life while wanting what everyone else has to fit in, be accepted, and feel a sense of belonging. Divine will asks us to trust intuitive guidance and step onto the road less traveled and unknown. God's will asks us to let go of earthly desires to follow His truth as our higher truth. Until we surrender, we know not what the higher truth is. It is God's path for us that creates our ultimate happiness, joy, freedom, and power.

To use free will correctly, we must choose divine will to achieve the Soul's destiny path. Only God and one's Soul knows what that path is. The mind cannot figure it out. Choosing ego will creates struggles and disappointments, leading to loss of faith and trust in the Universe. This brings us back to creating from the ego, which always diverts the Soul's true path. Controlling an outcome takes enormous effort and eventually becomes a burden. Or it will be limited in some way, or it will not create Soul fulfillment.

Contemplating His words, I realized I had two minds about raising children. There was no doubt I'd be an extraordinary mom filled with love. Even though uncertainty crept in during the adoption process, I dismissed it as normal anticipation. The curiosity of being a true healer was also knocking at my door, and this touched a deeper yearning within my Soul. Two paths presented themselves, and now I had to choose. Would I choose the safer, more conventional path or the unknown path?

I struggled with this decision for several weeks, and then sat with Lou to discuss the issue. He was unaware I had conversations with God, although at times I mentioned receiving guidance from spirit guides. "Lou, we've tried for a while to conceive. We've even explored adoption, yet I am confused about which road to take. What is the right choice for us?"

Lou's responses were always calm, and well thought out before answering. He was quiet. I waited patiently for his response. "I just want you to be happy. Whatever the outcome, I want you to be happy. We have the financial resources, a home in a good neighborhood and school district, there's no doubt a child would do well here. Maybe it's not up to us."

Words of wisdom were spoken. I learned something about him in that moment. Perhaps he had already mastered the ability to let go and let God, as I had been learning all these years. I became pensive, reflecting on his words, and the word of God several weeks ago. "Maybe you're right Lou."

After much reflection and meditation in the little blue room, I realized the conventional yearning for a child was present, but now the yearning for my Soul to express itself in full form was beginning to override the traditional human life path. I remembered the angel clouds and the words of the master guide. Releasing my attachment to the outcome of how I thought my life should be lived enabled me to completely surrender to an unknown, yet exciting path ahead. When we attach to a certain outcome, we limit our potential for even greater possibilities to manifest. Long ago I asked God to guide me on how to live life. My request to be shown the way forward was being granted.

Coming to grips with the truth in my Soul the next morning, I stood in front of the glass patio door and stared up at a cloudy sky. With arms stretched up to the universe, I cried out to God, "If I cannot be their mother, then I ask for all of these children to be adopted into loving homes! This, I ask of You, dear God! This, I ask of You!"

Tears streamed down my face as I gathered the paperwork still strewn on the dining room table, and ripped it into shreds. Feeling guilty for each child, I repeated, "I'm sorry I cannot be your mother. I'm sorry, so sorry. God's will is the truth. Please forgive me for not being your mother. I love you and will pray for you all."

My heart broke as I followed the will of God without understanding completely why I was doing so. Something miraculous occurred through this experience. As my heart broke, it was also lifted higher into the light of God's will and divine love. Another yearning came forth.

The next day, the sky was a beautiful shade of blue. I looked out the window speaking directly to God and said aloud, "I now surrender to the will of the divine, and ask to be shown the way forward to live as my Soul, and create the things my Soul needs to fulfill its destiny." The words flowed out of my mouth without a prior thought. My Soul had spoken.

A generous donation was given to the adoption agency. Within one year, every child was adopted.

My innate mothering abilities were meant to be used in a different way. It was time to truly learn how to love myself, to be mother Earth, to love, nurture, and help heal the wounds of humanity. Letting go of an Earth plane desire expanded my being into spirit. This was the most challenging surrender I had or would ever experience in life. Our ancestral programming to procreate for purposes of survival of the species can override other paths of higher fulfillment. We have yet to understand how to create from the Soul for all of humanity to live in balance with nature and the Universe. Every area of our lives is out of balance to some degree.

A new client was referred to me. She was attractive and married with four children. Her home was located in an exclusive part of town overlooking the Long Island Sound. Her husband was very successful, and other than being a mom to her four children, she was sadly discontent.

Our first session exposed her feelings. "I'm the wife of a wealthy man. He's good to me and loves me. I don't have to work, and I have live-in help. My children are my life, and I thought having them would fulfill all my dreams. I feel guilty in saying that despite all that I have, I am profoundly unhappy." Her statement was an eye-opener and deeply honest.

"What's missing is you, your sense of self, and your relationship with your Soul. Are you grateful for all that you have?" I asked.

"Yes, I'm very grateful, but I can't shake the unhappy feelings that fill my daily life."

We began the inward journey to learn how she needed to love herself. Oddly, she didn't continue sessions with me. I sensed she wasn't yet ready to learn how to love herself, and that staying in her unhappy state of mind would somehow play out over time. I hoped at some point she would wake up to the self-love needed to obtain her true source of fulfillment.

A seamstress at a local dry cleaner started a conversation with me about having and raising children. I had known her for many years, and we often chatted about her grandchildren.

"When are you going to have children, Pauline?"

"I'm not sure I am. I thought about adoption, but I believe my life is meant to be something different."

"Better to have kids of your own," she said with a dismissive wave. "You don't want to adopt. You'd have to work too hard to teach the kid your way of doing things."

I smiled and shook my head, not bothering to correct her misconceptions about adoption. I just wished her a good day, walked out of the store, and wondered, *What is my way? And would it be better than the way of someone else? Is my way so good that it won't create dysfunction?* I concluded that we have a long way to go to raise children to be their best selves. We must heal ourselves, including our ancestry.

In time, I began to see why I was not meant to raise children in this life. The destined transformation and higher path could not lend itself to creating a family in ordinary life. Children need a lot of attention, love, rearing, and teaching, and this would be a distraction from the deep awakening my Soul longed for. Understanding who I was created to be, and the existence of my life, started to become clear. I was not here on Earth to live an ordinary life, to gain approval from others, or to fit into a commonly accepted life path. I was here to undergo a massive transformation of the wounded ego into the Soul for the purposes of evolution of humankind.

Our Creator has endowed us with one of our greatest gifts as human beings: the ability to create human life. To understand what this means, I believe a person must have a good sense of self in order to be a good guide for a child. A parent must understand who his or her child is, not who the parent wants the child to be. At the time of our births, the planets are in some kind of alignment. Understanding what this alignment is through a natal or birth chart drawn up by a qualified astrologer is a good idea. I had planned to incorporate this understanding into motherhood to provide glimpses of my child's life and how I might better assist that child to be the best version of himself or herself.

God has an extraordinary plan for your life. Are you courageous enough to surrender to the inherent greatness of your Soul?

To Thine Own Self Be True

When we embrace the love of God inside ourselves toward our selves, we reach a level of enlightenment. Ultimately there is no greater love than that of self with Creator. As we embark on the path of awakening the Soul, we find the greatest love of all is found inside the self. The journey into our Soul is exactly this: to love thyself is to embody the Soul's energy while accepting the limitation of the human being as the impetus and catalyst to awaken.

At this point in my life, one thing became unequivocally clear. All desires and longings were a reflection of the truest desire of all, to reconnect with Soul and God as my source of love. There isn't enough love in the world, and every longing and desire from the wounded ego is the desire to return to love itself.

Within the silence of meditation and healing is an extraordinary connection of remembrance to our Soul. As the feelings of remembrance grow strong, every cell of the human and energy bodies rises to a higher vibration, bringing love into every area of our lives. Expressing that to the world in the form of unconditional love, compassion, tolerance, and connectedness with all life-forms will change how life is lived on Earth.

The most sacred relationship of all is with self as the foundation for all other relationships. Awakening Soul love will heal disease; bring inner peace, prosperity, abundance, and purpose; create loving relationships; and develop creativity, success, and fulfillment. Feeling complete from within radiates outward into the human matrix of Souls offering the same experience for others. Through the embodiment of Soul-love, feelings of confidence, trust, and wholeness grow strong. Loneliness does not exist here. We learn to look inward and upward for our truth and guidance rather than outward. Looking outward for answers will be someone else's truth. Believe you are a powerful co-creator when following the will of God.

From childhood, we have not been taught how to develop a relationship with our selves. Focusing on self was perceived as selfish. We have been taught to ignore self and focus on others for this makes us a good person. What kind of person are we without a relationship with self? We are empty, lonely, and controlling. We are plugged into other people as our sources of love, safety, and security. Controlling others and our environment for survival purposes is old-paradigm behavior.

As human beings we need each other to help us through difficult times. But without the connection to God or self, we can become dependent on those people to support us. Needing to lean on other people regularly will not awaken your Soul. How will you learn to become whole if you are plugged into others as your source? This outworn method of survival fades away as recognition of Soul self emerges.

You can't be true to Soul or God if you don't know who your Soul is. Being true to your Soul is the ultimate act of self-love. Then the love of God will work through you as a loving conduit to bring divine love and healing into the world.

I yearned for more love within and delved into my subconscious to find it. The longings were strong. Every desire I had, be it ego or Soul, led the way to my awakening through total surrender.

>*I sit in the little blue healing room in a blue swivel chair, candles lit to consecrate deeper healing, and a box of tissues on the desk behind me. I close my eyes, grounding my energy, and call in my guide. I quickly fall into the shadow of my inner world.*
>
>*Gently, I begin to feel the longing for more love. I fall into a trance. The yearning feels strong. Why is there not enough love in the world? Feelings of sadness surface. There is not enough love in the world or in my life. My eyes begin to tear up. I feel the longing for deep spiritual love and begin to cry. I feel no such love exists in the world and cry more deeply for humanity. How will we ever become unified with each other in the name of love?*
>
>*Then the image of Jesus enters my mind.*
>
>*I would love to make love to Jesus. Making love to God would be the ultimate experience in love. How beautiful an experience this would be. I cry at the thought of the beauty of it all and the lack of beauty in my inner world. I begin to feel a desire to make love to Jesus and realize what I want is to feel loved by God, to be in God's presence and feel worthy of it.*
>
>*I feel a desire to be vulnerable, open, to receive divine love. I realize my heart has not been open enough to the purity of God's love. Despite my awakening, my heart has not been capable of handling the pure energy of divine love. A huge ball of white, glistening light appears in my mind's eye. It is God, Universe, Source. I ask to be loved and to be embraced. I feel embarrassed and ashamed because*

how could I—a limited, unworthy human, inferior mortal—ask to be loved completely by God? I cry in shame and humiliation. Energy purges directly from my heart and solar plexus as I grieve for feeling embarrassed of my longing and emotions.

Words from my wounded ego speak: "You do not feel worthy of God's love." Deeply grieving, my mind keeps repeating, I am not worthy of God's love. After repeating the phrase over and over again, somehow, I do not feel that way anymore. Something shifts. I start to feel worthy of love and everything God wants for me. I am releasing subconscious beliefs that I feel unworthy of divine love. Am I beginning to love and honor me in the name of my Creator? Then all is quiet, and the crying stops.

Coming back into my body, I lay down on the healing table and allowed many healing spirits to transmit energy to release residual emotions. Feeling wiped out, I surrendered totally to the experience while lying on my back with arms outstretched. I speak aloud, "Dear spirit guides, angels, and God, please be with me. Heal me, release the limitations of mind and body to awaken my Soul." I fell back into trance.

Instantly energy moves in and around my body. Sensations of warmth, cool tingling, pulsations, and being lifted off the table are present. It feels wonderful as it moves from my toes into my legs, tingling throughout my entire body. A natural smile forms, and then I feel an energy open up from within that I had never felt before—the energy of pure beauty. Internal beauty from God, Goddess, Mother Earth, nature, love, and all things pure and innocent wake up. The feeling of oneness, being

connected to all life, human, animal, insect, trees,
sky, and ocean merged within my energy system.
Beauty of the divine mother, divine father, nature,
Universe, and I become one being.

The energy of internal beauty is whole, complete,
and pure. I feel connected to universal beauty. A few
moments later I feel goddess-like. My Soul makes
itself known and speaks, "I am Ishtar, your Soul
name."

Energy flows through my body from head to
toe, like currents of water surging down a wild river.
I feel sexy, beautiful, unconditionally loving, and
creative. An array of brilliant colors sweeps through
my mind; violet and red change to hues of orange
and yellow; a vibrant emerald green light bursts
into my mind, and I see the Emerald City of Oz.
Then all I can see is a white light that glistens like
a snowcapped mountain in sunlight. The white light
grows large, and I become one with it again. To my
amazement, I feel pure and cleansed as old wounds
wash away. Within seconds an enlightened heart
opens wide, capable of handling the great energy
of divine love. Creator allows me to merge with it
as a remembrance of who my Soul is created to be.
Never before had I felt anything so beautiful and at
the same time powerful. Never before had I felt solid
and complete from within myself.

Upon returning I realized the deep purges were necessary to
open the gateway to the destiny of my Soul. The feelings were beyond
what humans might consider regular feelings of beauty and love.
The full potential as a healer and light-worker was emerging, but I
wasn't yet aware of what this actually meant. The inherent God-given
divinity was pushing through the cracks of old wounds. All longings,

desires, and yearnings were about reconnection to Soul love, our one true love with God. I am one with God. I am love.

Forgiveness for Freedom

Deep healing work requires forgiveness. The act of forgiveness is a journey. Sometimes we forgive easily, other times not so easily. Forgiveness can be one of the most challenging spiritual actions we accomplish, especially when we have been deeply wounded by others, ourselves, or life. Yet it is the act of forgiveness that raises our vibrations, not only to set us free in this life, but to transcend the point of origin in our past lives where the karma originated between us and them. All hurtful situations are karmic, meaning we've been here before, and the behavioral pattern is repetitive in some way. The difference now is that we have the tools and understanding to forgive ourselves and others, releasing the karmic bonds with that person or group. From this healing place we no longer need to repeat damaging circumstances in this life or the next. This is especially true in abusive relationships.

This does not mean we continue a relationship with an abusive or toxic person. More than likely, disconnection from an abusive relationship will need to happen in order to heal, awaken, and embrace forgiveness. When we forgive the situation or person(s), cut the karmic bonds, which also positively affects our ancestors and future generations, we set ourselves free. When we love ourselves, we recognize the lessons on both sides and forgive all concerned with compassion.

My mind wandered back in time to the male friend who secretly harassed me with midnight phone calls in hopes of manipulating my feelings for him. At that time his request for forgiveness went unfulfilled. Now, as a healed woman, I could forgive him. Looking back, he was a troubled individual, yet I had attracted him into my life. On some level I, too, was troubled. Not in the same way as he, but the mirror of this friendship became clear. In my heart I forgave him, and felt free from the past.

Forgiving yourself can be more challenging than forgiving another. I recognized all of my past experiences required some degree of self-forgiveness. Perhaps I ignored red flags, perhaps I thought I could save someone, perhaps I was insensitive and lacked compassion. Whatever the case, little by little I saved myself through forgiveness, learned the lesson, and worked hard not to repeat history. The answer was to learn how to love myself, first through healing, and then though self-acceptance.

Conclusion: Love yourself intensely and wholly, and you won't feel the lack of anything in your life. If you only knew how much divine love you were created with, you'd never worry about anything ever again. Releasing attachment to all things will be easy when you have the ability to love unconditionally. Love is the magnet to abundance.

CHAPTER 8

THE SOUL'S DESTINY PATH

Surrendering as I did opened the pathway for the Soul's destiny to be awakened. There's a difference between walking a spiritual path and walking a destiny path. Some people believe destiny is about being successful or purposeful in the world. I see destiny as an awakening of who we were created to be at the Soul level and then following an unknown path to be in service to the world as directed by God. Most likely the Soul's service isn't known to the conscious mind because it doesn't necessarily mean engaging in your God-given strengths. Healing the darkness within and letting the Soul guide you to what it wants to do in this lifetime brings true purpose. With my God-given strengths, I thought I was to be a human resource director, yet I was led to an entirely different area to fulfill my Soul's purpose. Outer success isn't the goal, internal evolution is; becoming who you were created to be, is your highest purpose. Success isn't as much about what you do as it is about who you become.

A paradox exists here regarding how much control a person actually has over his or her life when choosing destiny. Since destiny of a Soul cannot be figured out or planned, faith and trust in God's plan will require a constant affair with surrender and the will to follow. Everyone has been programmed with a destiny path, but few will actualize it. Following the mystery of the unknown with faith and trust instead of control revealed my destiny. A Soul doesn't find destiny; destiny finds the Soul.

The power to create what the Soul desires will be strong with many options, yet the most fulfilling options will be chosen by the Soul, not the mind, and they won't be directed by financial gain, or fame. This does not mean being financially prosperous is out of the question. In fact, quite the opposite is true. When following the Soul's destiny, prosperity and abundance are already scripted in.

Deep internal desires within your heart are clues to fulfilling your yearnings. Keep in mind all desires are rooted in one true desire, to remember who you are as a Soul being. Continued expansion is necessary for evolution to occur. The key is to follow inner guidance until the result manifests as a dream come true. Sometimes I think we are kept in the unknowing phase so the outcome is a wonderful surprise. We must learn to become comfortable with uncertainty as faith and trust must be stronger than our fears.

When we use authentic power to create something, it benefits many people for that is the highest directive of your awakening. Our greatest achievements will be to understand how connected we are through the unity of our Souls.

Miracles of Energy Healing

Continued surrender and personal healing attracted more clients, expanding my healing practice. I became quite busy through referrals. My vessel had become a clear conduit for universal grace to flow through to help others learn how to heal themselves and awaken their Souls. Finally, my body was strong enough to maintain the energy of the divine to help others heal major life issues.

Miracles occurred through me, not by me, to help those afflicted with earthly disease, emotional wounds, or tragic circumstances. The Soul's power has the ability to heal any imbalance. In truth, the person who receives healing by the energy flowing through the vessel is the most powerful. You choose to heal or not. A healer is powerless over your condition, unless you are deeply willing to heal. I came to believe these principles as shown by the Universe: Love heals all wounds, forgiveness heals all karma, and compassion creates miracles.

The Soul is the healer of the wounded ego. The degree to which a person heals depends on readiness to move beyond the affliction. Sometimes the mind says, *Yes, I'm ready to heal,* but the subconscious says, *No, I'm stuck.* Digging deep into the subconscious is where true healing occurs. Only then is the issue uprooted and finally released.

Miracle 1

A young mother adopted a child of eighteen months. Shortly thereafter she was diagnosed with breast cancer. Within a few years, four brain tumors developed that couldn't be completely surgically removed due to their sizes. Several tumors were operated on to reduce their sizes in preparation for radiation treatment. The hope was radiation therapy would significantly reduce the size of the tumors, giving her more time to live. Doctors had no expectation that radiation would completely dissolve the tumors. I was asked to help. I alone could do nothing, but with God's help, I prayed a miracle would occur.

Intuitively I knew she needed to make more time for herself. This was part of why cancer had grown within her body. Lack of self-care and not enough time spent with her husband were causing frustration. I was guided by spirit to offer advice on how to create a daily ritual. She was to spend twenty minutes in prayer and meditation, morning and evening. My herbal stills kicked in, and I concocted a very strong antitumor, anticancer herbal preparation, which was to be taken three times daily to strengthen immunity and brain function. During the twenty-minute ritual she was to take the herbal formula, meditate, pray. The she was to turn her head upside down, envisioning the herb-infused blood rushing to the brain, dissolving the tumors. Since she did not live locally, we worked energetically by phone several times a week during the five weeks of radiation therapy. After five weeks of using various energy modalities, she had a brain scan. We all hoped the tumors had reduced in size. The brain scan revealed all tumors were completely gone. She was faithful to her daily routine and learned to ask for help from others. Doctors were perplexed by the outcome. We rejoiced at the miracle given by God's grace.

Miracle 2

A young man of nineteen years had witnessed his father's suicide. The father's plan was to take his own life along with his daughter and son by placing arsenic on pizza slices before sitting down to eat dinner. The father ate several slices and encouraged the children to eat. The daughter ate one slice. The young man wasn't hungry and didn't eat anything, noticing the cheese looked a bit curdled. The father kept encouraging him to eat, but the young man insisted he wasn't hungry. Shortly afterward, the father began to show signs of toxicity as his body began to fail. The sister began to feel ill. Not knowing what to do, the young man called his mother, who immediately instructed him to call 911. When paramedics arrived to assess the situation, the father had passed away. The sister needed immediate treatment and was rushed to the hospital.

After this incident, the young man went into suicidal depression, speaking about feeling alone, wanting to kill himself, and not understanding why his father would do such a thing. He was experiencing survivor guilt and kept talking about how he should have died with his father. There was a delay in working with a trauma therapist, and his mother begged me to help. I felt her terror for her son's life. What could I do to help? I'm not a trauma therapist. This was beyond my ability, yet intuitively I felt I should allow it. If God was bringing this boy to me, then God would surely be present.

The young man came for a session right away. As he told the story, I felt the pain and anguish he experienced and cried silently with compassion. Once he finished speaking, I gently asked him to lie down on the healing table. As soon as I opened up the energy, Jesus was present. I felt the power and love of a divine entity who revealed Himself to my mind's eye. Jesus stood in a long white gown, His brown hair touching His shoulders. A halo surrounded His head. His facial expression was gentle, exuding love, but He was not smiling. In fact, He appeared neutral.

"Do you believe in Jesus?" I asked.

"Yes I do," affirmed the boy.

The Deity's energy was powerful, guiding me, pushing me around the room like a ping-pong ball. I was but a vessel for Christ and had no control over what happened. The boy cried as he spoke, "I see Jesus! I see Him! I see Him! Why would He come to me? Am I not supposed to be dead?"

To his fragile mind, Jesus spoke. "Jesus is telling me I'm supposed to be alive, I'm loved, I'm worthy of God's love." He kept repeating these words as he cried.

I witnessed the young man's wonderment as Christ made Himself known. My heart opened as I recollected the feelings of love from my own divine healing sessions and bowed my head in reverence. He cried tears of anguish and torment; his body trembled as grief and depression were released. I was a bystander witnessing a miracle and cried in gratitude that God trusted me as a conduit through which He could work a miracle for the boy, his mother, and his sister.

The young man came out of the trance and opened his eyes. He was dazed but not confused. He slowly sat up and looked at me.

"How do you feel?" I asked.

He slowly and gently said, "I don't feel alone anymore. I don't want to kill myself. I'm so sorry I felt that way and worried my mother. I don't understand why this happened, but I'm okay now. I was lost, but I'm okay now."

The next day his mom called me to validate the miracle. Her son had been healed by divine intervention. Her daughter was recovering in the hospital. I was in awe and had no words to offer but these: "We thank God for the miracle of healing and life."

Miracle 3

The young landscaper had been bitten by a tick a year prior to seeing me. His face had become slightly paralyzed on the right side from the toxic bite. Most likely he had Lyme disease, which was treated with an antibiotic at the time. Nothing further was done to treat the illness. A tick bite releases a toxin into the bloodstream, which in time affects the central nervous system, potentially causing paralysis. I believed this was what had happened.

The corner of his right eye and mouth drooped. I grabbed a tissue and wiped drool from the right corner of his lips as he lay on the healing table. He was Hispanic and didn't speak English. Quickly remembering my Spanish language skills, I asked him to tell me what happened. "Qué pasó?" I questioned. He spoke using the word *garrapata*, which I had to look up in the dictionary. The word "tick" in Spanish is *garrapata*. The healing began as energy started to run through my hands as I placed them in various places around his head and body. His right eye began to tear. As I repeated over and over, "Releasing the toxin from the garrapata," water streamed out of the right eye.

I needed a spot of his blood, and asked him to prick his finger using a sterile lancet. This technique is used to detoxify a toxin from the blood. On the body are acupressure points, one of them being a detox point. I placed the spot of blood on a Q-tip in a small baggie and placed it on the point. After forty minutes of treatment, his face began to change. A slight restoration of the right side of his face was visible. The healing was now complete. He sat up and I pointed at the mirror, for him to take a look at his face. He observed his face. "Muy bueno! Muy bueno!"

I nodded. We finished, and I asked him to stop by my home in two days to assess the results of the healing.

On seeing him after two days, I was delighted to see his face had returned to normal without any sign of paralysis. He smiled with joy, pointed to his face, and said, "Gracias, señora. Gracias mucho."

"De nada, Manolo," I replied. Again, being in awe of how God was working through me, I bowed my head and then looked up at the sky. "Thank You, God, for Your grace."

Miracle 4

A man in his twenties contacted me to ask for help in hope of curing genital herpes. I was hesitant to respond. Cure herpes? How could such a virus be cured? My thoughts drifted back to the woman who had four brain tumors. Anything is possible when God is involved. Surely it is not I who performed healing miracles but God who worked miracles through His conduits and the readiness of a client's Soul. I was honest with the man. "I can't promise you'll be healed, but if you are willing to try, I will ask God to help us."

"I'm all in," said the man.

The first thing I was guided to do was create a strong herbal program to reduce stress and increase immunity with many antiviral herbs. My spirit guides whispered instructions in my ear on how to proceed once herbal medicine was in place. Monthly sessions were needed to address the emotional, mental, and spiritual aspects of why he attracted herpes. He was delightfully open. I enjoyed listening to his honesty as he described many unhealthy situations he engaged in. At times we even laughed as in hindsight, his destructive behavior became clear, and he vowed to change. In addition, when the virus was active with infection, I was to see him immediately to detox the virus from his system using energy medicine.

After each energy detox when the virus was active, we noticed the healing response lessened the infection time by a day or two. Over time, we noticed the length of time between infections was longer and longer. Feeling positive about our work together, we pushed on with hope and continued for the next several years.

The last time I saw him the infection was very mild, yet present. He remained open and hopeful as I witnessed a touching transformation that often brought tears to my eyes. Lying on the table, the young man closed his eyes and began to pray. The energy started to run through me as I felt extreme heat in my body. I was in the presence of a most powerful being. Again Jesus made himself known. Seeing a vision of Him in my mind's eye, I was humbled to my knees. I was not guided to ask this man if He believed in Jesus. It didn't matter. Jesus was there.

Kneeling as I was, it was my job to hold space for a miracle to occur. Again I was but a vehicle through which God could work. At one point, Jesus lifted me up as if to say, *No need to kneel.* I stood at the bottom of the healing table with arms stretched out, just as Jesus would do. God's energy flowed through me into the room like a powerful wave of love. I cried as I felt ultimate compassion for this man who desperately wanted to heal his life and this condition he had been living with for many years.

The next day I received a phone call. "Hey, Pauline, the sores are completely gone! They are gone! Man, they are gone." He spoke with excitement. My heart skipped a beat. Could this really be true?

"I'm overjoyed for you!" I replied. "God works miracles. Thank God, stay in the Light, keep healing, and keep me posted please."

Every now and again I'd receive a message on my answering

machine from him. "Hey, just letting you know I'm still clean. No outbreaks or anything. I can't thank you enough." And every time I heard his voice speak those words, a tear would roll down my face. "Thank You, God, for trusting me to help Your child." I believe he was healed because he owned his wounds, his insecurities, and he was true to his vow to change his actions. Maintaining a spiritual practice was necessary to remain healthy. The power is within us to heal any condition we have attracted into our lives. The journey is deep, yet possible.

It's been over fifteen years, and every time I hear him say, "I'm still clean with no outbreaks," I am touched more deeply by the love of our Creator, who only wants the best for us.

Miracle 5

A beautiful woman in her early forties contacted me asking for help. She had a serious condition involving a calcification that had formed around the facial nerve on the right side of her face. The stone caused many unsettling side effects including, pain, hearing loss, the inability to swallow or produce salvia, and malfunction of the submandibular gland. Her speech had become slurred, and she had a staph infection with swollen glands in the neck. Doctors warned the calcification was traveling toward the brain and there was a ninety percent chance an aneurysm would form, or possible cardiac arrest could occur as she waited for surgery to be scheduled within three months-time. The prognosis was if she was still alive, and made it through surgery, she would have facial paralysis, loss of taste, a permanent port in her neck, and a speech impediment.

I agreed to try to help. She lived an hour away, but I was guided to see her immediately in person for the first visit. Somehow she managed to drive herself to my home in desperation, despite having an active staph infection. I felt no fear about coming in contact with the infection. She was spiritually aware and believed angels had been with her as she drove the distance.

The session began, and intuitively I saw what was going on her life. I gently brought up relationship issues. I guided her back into childhood to heal the old wounds still living within her energy field. Her inner child needed to feel loved and to feel worthy. The little girl in her needed to be seen and heard. Wounds from long ago needed attention, and healing. She cried throughout the session. I, too, had cried throughout my first healing session as old wounds surfaced, but I also knew a healing had begun for her.

The next day she called to say the staph infection was completely gone, and somehow she felt more positive about herself. Regardless of how powerful a healer is, you never quite get used to how miracles occur. There is always a feeling of being in awe and deep gratitude for the gift of healing which always includes our Soul, and God.

Our work was not finished. The calcification had to be dealt with. Surgery to remove the growth was scheduled in a few weeks, but not without severe danger. The surgeon stressed that there was no guarantee the stone could be removed without permanent damage. The submandibular gland also needed to be removed. She and her family were terrified by the prognosis. And so was I.

She explained her fears of not being able to live the life she so passionately loved. I felt intuitively God would work through me. How? I did not know. Trust was my guidance. If God sent a person to me, then I must trust that God will work through me. Regular phone conversations were set up to transmit energy healing in hope of somehow healing the calcification.

As we spoke over the phone, I felt my Soul split into two beings. One part of me was in my body; the other part had telepathically joined the client in her location. I saw myself standing over her with many other beings of light and angels. Images of the calcification or stone wrapped around the nerve in her face began to appear. Energy was being transmitted to her through me from afar, yet I was also with her.

The night before surgery was the most profound healing session. This was the third session over the phone. After a few minutes she said, "Lots of saliva is forming in my mouth."

My spirit guide spoke through me. "Don't swallow it. Spit it out." Saliva kept flowing, and she kept spitting it out for about ten minutes longer. Then she said, "Oh gosh, I feel grit in the saliva, like rough sand in my mouth, and my hearing seems to have improved."

"Keep spitting it out," I replied. This continued for another ten to twenty minutes.

In my mind's eye, I saw the stone crack in half, into the shape of a triangle. "Oh my God, I think the stone has cracked and fallen away from the nerve! I see a triangle shape, and I think it is dissolving! I think this is what you are experiencing," I exclaimed.

"My mouth is full of grit, and it's terribly uncomfortable. But something just happened." She sounded like her tongue was coated with sand.

"I feel we should stop now. Is there a way you can schedule an X-ray of the stone before surgery tomorrow?" I asked.

"Yes absolutely! I will request an X-ray tomorrow before surgery. I will call the surgeon now, and make sure of it!" She was as convinced as I was that something incredible had occurred.

The next morning the brain surgeon spoke with her at bedside in the hospital. "I got your message for another X-ray because you believe the stone has cracked into pieces? That's not possible," said the doctor.

"Not possible isn't in my vocabulary!" She spoke with authority. Another X-ray was not granted.

As she was wheeled into surgery she loudly spoke for everyone in the room to hear her words, "The stone has broken into pieces. I will not have facial paralysis or a speech impediment. Nor will I have a permanent port in my neck and I'm definitely not going to lose my taste buds. None of these things are going to happen to me because of Pauline!" One of the surgeons looked at the other surgeons and said, "Who is Pauline?"

The surgery went better than expected. The submandibular gland was saved while the mess of broken calcified pieces which had fallen away from the facial nerve took quite some skill to clean out. Every word she spoke before surgery came true! We were flabbergasted by the miracle. Faith, belief, and the deep desire to heal creates miracles we can't even fathom.

The surgeons were very perplexed and questioned what she had been doing. "What did you tell them?" I giggled. "I told him it's none of his business, and he wouldn't believe me if I told him." She, too, giggled.

For years to come she and I would cry over the miracle of this healing. I couldn't imagine such a young beautiful woman living with the original prognosis for the rest of her life, and in gratitude to God, she did not.

Miracle 6

A woman came to me desperately wanting to become pregnant. After several attempts at in vitro fertilization, doctors determined the husband had slight damage to the male Y chromosome, resulting in the eggs not being fertilized. She and I scheduled several sessions leading up to the next in vitro appointment, which was a few months away. During each session I felt her pain of not being able to conceive. My heart broke for her.

During the final session, which was scheduled the week of the next in vitro appointment, an incredible thing happened. While I was working with her energy to raise the vibration of her eggs to hold fertilization, her husband's soul entered the healing. Her husband was physically at home, watching TV.

I began to see an image of a Y chromosome and where it was slightly defective. Spirit showed me how to repair the chromosome using energy. I brushed over the damaged area with light energy, like using a paintbrush over and over to cover the area thoroughly.

Following the guidance of spirit, I repeated brushing over the chromosome until I was guided to stop. Then I observed how its shape began to change, into a stronger image. I had never done this before, nor had I learned such a thing was possible, especially because we were dealing with a congenital defect. Somehow I was shown how to connect her eggs with his sperm, which now had a healthy Y chromosome. At the end of the session she said, "I feel new energy inside my body. It's different. I'm lighter. Will I become pregnant?"

"Let's pray and hope so," I replied. I never liked that question. Giving false hope was not what I wanted to do.

The session ended.

When she arrived home that night, she called to say her husband had felt energy in his pelvic area during the hour we were in session. I knew something miraculous had occurred.

After the next in vitro procedure, she called to say every egg was fertilized and healthy. "This is wonderful news! What will you do with all these fertilized eggs?" I asked.

"We have decided to implant only one egg. The eggs are healthy, and we feel it's best to go slowly."

We hung up the phone. There was no further contact until about a year later, when she sent a photo of a beautiful baby girl, dressed in the most adorable pink outfit with matching bonnet. I texted her with my deepest wishes for a happy, healthy family. My heart felt warmed, and I thanked God for the miracle that was granted.

We never spoke again. Our contract had been fulfilled.

From Heaven to Earth

During the seven years of graceful isolation, I had been floating around higher dimensions of reality. Nothing triggered me. I felt whole, loved, and supported. To me, every person was beautiful. Although I was able to observe their shadow side, I felt love for them in a humanitarian way. I was filled with light, and so often people would comment on how my eyes seemed filled with a sparkling light. I'd respond, "Oh, just meditate, and your eyes will sparkle too."

> *One day in 2009, while I was meditating, the voice spoke, "It is time for you to return." Jolted out of meditation by the words, I questioned, "Return to where?"*
>
> *"It's time to return to Earth reality. The experiences from which you have healed and grown will be your teachings. Many are now becoming ready." Said the Voice.*
>
> *"I don't want to return. I'm happy, peaceful, and safe. Am I not doing as you have guided?" The voice did not respond.*
>
> *Again I say," I don't want to return! Please don't hurt me. I'm afraid to return to the Earthly world where people are filled with hate and lack of understanding."*
>
> *I was crying, repeating in my mind, Please don't make me go back. Please don't make me go back.*

Yet in the days, weeks, and months following God's request, I found myself beginning to slip back into the third-dimensional Earth reality, which took several years to completely ground back into. Living in the energy of inner peace, and love for so many years became the foundation of strength upon which I could return to the ego world and maintain inner balance as the world evolved.

Soul Greatness

When we embrace the part of the self that is divine—the Soul—we will create a level of greatness for humanity to allow all living things to live in peace, harmony, and abundance.

Have you ever wondered how it is possible to be alive? How it is possible that you are able to breathe, walk, talk, think, cry, eat, dance, play, or feel love? What makes your heart beat with life and aliveness? The infinite energy of your Soul enables your body to be alive, your mind to think, your heart to love. The Soul houses your physical body, giving it life, breath, and love. Every organ and cell of your flesh and bones is alive due to the life-force energy of the Soul. Pure in nature, your spirit is a vast living consciousness that is eternal, and it longs for your remembrance.

Think of your Soul as a consciousness and a metaphysical energy. Since the Soul is not physical energy, like a tree or an animal, you can't physically see it. Through your senses, you can feel it. This living consciousness has many layers of energy bodies and vortexes that transmit and receive energy. Although an evolved trained eye can see the shimmer of the layers of color that configure your energy system, it is not visible to most people with an untrained eye. Kirlian photography is a special type of photography that can capture the Soul's layers of energy, which can then be seen in a photograph.

I will briefly explain the design of the layers of energy bodies and energy centers, or chakras that comprise the Soul as it exists around the human body. This is a simplistic explanation solely for visual imagery. I'll start with the human body and then move outward, extending several feet beyond the physical body.

First there exists a human physical body composed of cellular matter. Without the Soul present, your body would be a cold, lifeless casing. Immediately surrounding the physical body is the etheric body, which contains a blueprint of all lifetimes. This body is seen as a white shimmering mist that surrounds the physical body. The blueprint contains memory of all experiences and all lifetimes, including the point of our Soul's creation and highest purpose. Karmic and ancestral experiences, patterns, and issues are held here. Sometimes the etheric body is explored by going into a past life to heal a current chronic life issue or to observe the future.

The emotional body sits atop the etheric body and extends out about one foot. This body is responsible for managing your feelings and emotions, ranging from fear to love, and can be seen as an array of colors. When we feel peaceful, the color blue or green will be present. When we feel fearful, the color red might show up. When your emotional body becomes blocked by emotions such as anger, grief, and guilt, physical illness or pain can be present. This body is one of the most powerful energy bodies because it is directly related to our physical health. Our emotions are our greatest assets to be used to awaken to the Soul and its primary emotion—love. If we want to feel love at its deepest, purest level, we must connect with the Soul through the emotional body.

The pain body in my view is somewhere in-between or mixed in with the emotional, etheric, and physical bodies. Pain can be caused by emotions, thoughts or beliefs, karma from past lives, or show up physically. When this body is opened up, various types of pain are felt. We have been taught to suppress the pain body, but as you've read in this book, it is necessary to heal our deep wounds that reflect pain from the past. For very sensitive people, it is challenging to heal this body, and many are not ready to delve into it. Pain is the absence of love.

Moving outward from the emotional body is the mental body, which governs your thought patterns, belief systems, analyzing abilities, and logic. It also extends out about one foot beyond the emotional body. The mental body is another powerful body because through your thought patterns and belief systems, you create your life by evolving or remain stuck in old ways of living. A thought pattern such as *I can't have abundance* will keep you stuck, whereas a thought pattern such as *I attract and create abundance because I am worthy* will create abundance. Soul thought patterns are positive and empowering. Acknowledging limited thought patterns can be challenging because many of the thought patterns that keep us stuck are subconscious.

A beautiful variety of colors—including red, orange, yellow, green-blue, violet, and turquoise—comprise the emotional and mental bodies. Each color represents a specific energy, emotion, thought pattern, and life experience, and will change over time. When your Soul incarnates into the physical body, the mental, emotional, and etheric bodies are activated to accommodate our human personality and forthcoming life. As these bodies of energy are activated, the wounded ego develops as negative emotions, and beliefs are assimilated from hurtful experiences as well as brought in from prior lives. For example, let's say someone is angry for no apparent reason and can't identify why he or she feels angry. When looking back at childhood or other areas of the individual's life, the trigger still can't be found. In this case, it's likely the emotion was brought in from a past life. Children can be born with strong emotions from prior lifetimes. Past-life healing may be needed to uncover the trigger.

The outermost energy body is the intuition body, which is furthest from the physical body and sits atop the mental body. It is responsible for psychic energy and knowingness. This magnificent body is like radar. It has the ability to know and sense things before they happen; it is a body of pure psychic energy. Have you ever gotten a bad feeling about something, and then it turned out just as you felt it would? Have you ever gotten a great feeling about something, and it turned out just as you felt it would? Intuition is very closely related to your emotions because we usually intuit through our feelings rather than our thoughts. You can't think intuition; you can only feel it. This body of energy can usually be seen as a violet or white light extending three feet from the physical body. This is our strongest body, yet it is the least developed. Developing this energy body creates feelings of empowerment and peace.

You have experienced the intuition body many times despite its cryptic nature. The biggest emotional blocks in knowing the intuitional body are fear and doubt. The biggest mental block in knowing the intuitional body is the thought that it does not exist. Not everyone allows this body to operate and flow naturally as it was designed to do. You and everyone around you are naturally psychic! It is a God-given gift. Everyone has experienced psychic energy at one time or another without realizing that they were in the flow of "knowingness."

Chakras, or energy centers, also conduct energy and are connected to the energy bodies. There are seven main chakras and many more in and around the body. Here is a brief explanation of each main chakra, starting at the base of the spine.

The first is the root chakra, which sits at the base of the spine. Its color is red, and its main function is to keep the Soul grounded in the body and connected to the Earth. The issues this chakra governs are survival, immune system, blood, bones, manifestation. The blockage of this center is fear.

The second is the sacral chakra, which sits just below the navel. Its color is orange, and its main function is to use life-force energy to create, procreate, prosper, and use power wisely. Emotions flow through this energy center. The blockages of this center are guilt and shame.

The third is the solar plexus chakra, which sits just below the breastbone. Its color is yellow, and its main function is to develop a relationship with self and self-worth and purpose in the world. In fact, this is the chakra where the Soul awakens! The blockages of this center are intimidation and self-doubt.

The fourth is the heart chakra, which sits between the breasts. Its color is green or pink, and its main function is to express love, compassion, and forgiveness. It is connected to our outer relationships. The blockage is this center is anger or fear of being hurt.

The fifth is the throat chakra, and it sits in the throat area. Its color is sky-blue, and its main function is to speak, to express from the heart, and to follow the will of God. Our unique voice develops here. This center also enables us to listen to others. The blockages of this center are lies and using ego desires to express and create.

The sixth is the brow chakra, or third eye. It sits in the center of the forehead. Its color is violet, and its main function is to see truth without judgment. This is the psychic center of intuition and clairvoyance. The blockage of this center is believing the illusion of Earth life.

The seventh is the crown chakra and it sits above the head. Its color is white, and its main function is to connect us with God, our Soul, spirits, and to trust the process of life, allowing true freedom. The blockage of the center is attachment.

These energy bodies and chakras are responsible for giving out and receiving energy. When they are open and flowing, we feel balanced, well, and energized. When they are blocked, we feel ill, tired, and out of sync.

Your spirit is flawless electromagnetic energy that encompasses unconditional love, compassion, kindness, greatness, gentleness, forgiveness, confidence, joy, peace, abundance, psychic energy, power, wisdom, health, creativity, and freedom. Within your Soul is a mainframe of information that pertains specifically to you. This ageless being spans all your human lifetimes—past, present, and future—as well as eternal life when you are in pure spirit. It knows all your karma and your highest potential as a human being. All the answers to the questions you seek, no matter how simple or challenging, reside within. Everything you need to know about yourself is within waiting to be explored. Your Soul has co-created a life with wonderful and challenging circumstances to be catalysts to awaken.

Soul is an electromagnetic energy that is part of a colossal energy that we call God, Source, Universe, Creator, All that Is, Infinite, and so on. It cannot be destroyed or altered. To the degree we can know of such things, this electromagnetic energy is very sensitive and acts like a magnet. It attracts in the patterns of thought and emotion you feel and believe. So if you think negative thoughts, you will attract negativity. If you feel angry on a regular basis, you will attract circumstances that feed anger. If your thought process is positive, you will attract positive circumstances. If you feel the love or empowerment within, you will attract the same.

The electromagnetic energy of your Soul is not like the electricity that powers your computer or cell phone or that lights up a bulb. In fact, this kind of energy disturbs the natural electromagnetic energy field of your Soul. In turn, this causes electromagnetic imbalances in the brain and physical body that can cause disease. Energy pathways are then blocked and rerouted through unnatural channels. It is predicted that the use of cell phones will cause brain dysfunction and many mysterious physical ailments in the future.

The electromagnetic energy of your Soul is similar to crystalline light-energy imagined as a ball of white light, sometimes seen with a blue flame in its center. Light energy is the most powerful healing energy source in the Universe. As my Soul awakened, my body began to absorb light energy into its cells. As this occurred, I noticed a slight reversal of the aging process. I began to look younger. I could exercise in the same rigorous workouts as when I was in my twenties. Oddly, I didn't need to exercise quite as strenuously. With twenty minutes of varied exercise programs of yoga, light weight lifting, dance, or brisk walking a few times a week, my body toned up quickly. I was amazed by this and acknowledged that as deeper healing occurred, my body evolved. I believe this was because the dense energy of negativity and karmic patterns were releasing from my Soul's mainframe or etheric body. No longer was I filled with heavy energy from the past. Eating healthfully and using natural cosmetics developed without animal testing seemed to give my skin a natural glow. There's a sparkle in the eye of a person who embodies the light of an eternal Soul.

Your Soul is an extension of God, and it has been created from the greatness of its parent. Just the way a child is an extension of its mother and father, the Soul is an extension of its Creator. Extension cords of energy flow through you and extend out of your head into the Universe, reconnecting you to original life-force energy. This is how your body is fueled and able to function on the physical level.

The universal life-force energy of the Creator feeds your Soul, and your Soul feeds your body.

All Souls are extensions of God, and collectively we make up one big collective Soul living on Earth. An individual Soul—such as Jesus or Gandhi—can impact the world greatly. As a collective of Souls, we have the power to transform our world into the most loving, beautiful, peaceful, abundant place to live! The degree to which we live in peace, love, and harmony depends on the degree to which we have acknowledged the Soul's greatness and power in co-creation with God.

We all share a sacred bond that began on the Soul plane and continues on the Earth plane from one lifetime to another. We are not separate from each other. Rather, we are all one and created from the same source of love. Have you never felt the pain or joy of another person you never met? Of course you have. Because we are all connected, we can feel the emotions of others through the collective energy of the Soul matrix.

Created from eternal light energy, your Soul is the powerhouse of inner healing ability. This powerful essence has the ability to heal everything, including disease, trauma, heartbreak, and grief. Every characteristic we strive for as human beings your Soul already is! The strongest yearning for all human beings is to remember our truths, God, and the divine plan that was created for each of us in the moment of our Soul's creation. All longings represent your need to be consciously reunited with God's love.

We could intellectualize the birthplace of the Soul as a dimension where Souls are born, where they return after death, and where they visit during sleep. Far beyond the boundaries of the Earth, let's imagine a plane of energy and white crystalline, golden light, and call it the Soul dimension. It is the natural birthplace and home to all Souls. Everything in this dimension is created of the purest, divine, crystalline, white-golden light.

While we sleep, the Soul returns home to be recharged by the love and wholeness of its Creator. Since the Soul is a powerful, multidimensional presence, it can be in many places at once—in part in your body while asleep, in part traveling home to be recharged, or traveling around the cosmos visiting with its true origin in other dimensions of the Universe.

Have you ever awakened and felt disoriented, not knowing where you are? Most likely a good part of your Soul has traveled to higher dimensions, and on waking, your Soul had not completely returned into your body. This usually happens when we feel stressed or are not giving our bodies enough rest. Once your Soul has anchored back into the body, awareness of your surroundings is restored, releasing the grogginess of sleep. This is a sign that you are probably overworked, stressed from daily Earth life, or in a deep phase of transformation and awakening. During this phase your Soul begins to travel to other dimensions to gather new and higher energy for you to assimilate. As you assimilate higher vibrations, your Soul radiates those energies out into the world. Whatever the case, the need for regular spiritual practices such as meditation, prayer, or connecting with nature, plants, or animals is crucial.

The human body is a dense entity, and it takes a lot of energy for the Soul to house our flesh and bones. So traveling to the Soul dimension every night is like going home to reconnect with love, wholeness, and wellness. The need to return to the Soul plane is like the need to quench your thirst on a hot, humid day.

As challenging as this may sound, your Soul chose the family you were born into. If you have a good relationship with your family, you feel blessed. If you don't have a good relationship with family, you are still blessed. For the reasons of healing karma, the Soul chooses its parents and other members to right the wrongs of a past-life experience. Forgiveness usually plays a big role here through understanding why you and certain people don't get along. Healing may occur, and the relationship changes to become a beautiful loving union. Or healing may occur, and the relationship dissolves, but the triggers are gone. Many people struggle with family problems, which are all karmic and destined. Look deeper into why the relationship is challenging. Heal yourself and awaken. Forgive, and karma will be released.

When the Soul enters the body for the first time through a developing spinal cord in utero, from the top of the head to the bottom of the spine, it facilitates life-force energy and consciousness. In that moment, the miracle of life has occurred; life is created. The moment there is a heartbeat from a fetus, the Soul is present. It is possible the heartbeat is active well before it is detected by an ultrasound. From this moment, the energy bodies are activated to accommodate human life.

The moment the heart stops beating (physical death), the Soul begins a process of shedding the physical body. The journey back home can be arduous. A body that can no longer sustain human life becomes an empty shell. As the spirit is leaving the body, it slowly moves up the spinal column from the bottom of the spine toward the head. We see this happening as a person nears death. First they lose the ability to walk as their legs become weak. Then the ability to control urine and bowel movements is lost. The desire to eat diminishes, the ability to speak is weakened, and finally, the heart stops beating as the Soul leaves through the top of the head. It is actually a beautiful process if you can see just how powerful the journey back into the spirit world is.

If a Soul is awakened, it will shed the human body upon physical death more easily because the yearning to return to heaven is strong. As ego is released, the spirit ascends to reunite with God. A Soul may linger on the Earth plane for a while before transcending into heaven, but not always. From my experiences, I've noticed a Soul usually stays earthbound until the funeral or ceremonial events are completed before returning home. Then Life continues in heaven, and the Soul knows exactly how to continue living without the human body. After all, your Soul is eternal, and your body is temporary. You have spent more time in the spirit world than on the Earth, so life is easily and naturally continued here. Your Soul does not need a body to exist. But your body needs a Soul to be alive.

When the body is shed on physical death, the Soul must begin a process of splitting off from the ego. Some Souls can get stuck in Earth plane energy if they died with strong emotions, such as fear or anger, or were very attached to material possessions. Or if they believed human life is the only life, then their attachment to the Earthly world may remain somewhat intact. The ego-based emotional and mental bodies are still operating and can cause delays in the journey home. It is important to pray for people who have died so they return home as quickly as possible. As we know, our departed loved ones will oversee our lives and contribute when they can to help us. Messages may come through many channels, including dreams, paying attention to metaphysical signs such as feathers or the appearance of a red cardinal, or through a psychic medium.

Scientists have believed that when we physically die, the consciousness dies with it. The point at which the heart stops beating is when all life perishes. Well interestingly, science is now beginning to recognize that although the physical body has died, a living consciousness still exists. They are beginning to recognize this phenomenon with machines that measure current and electricity. The human energy field is exactly that—an electromagnetic energy current. It continues to be alive long after the heart has stopped beating and the physical body decomposes.

The love of your Soul is so powerful it can change a negative vibration in a room filled with people simply by radiating love to everyone in it! I remember attending the wake of a young mother. Her death was tragic. The room was filled with grief-stricken people. I felt deep sadness and despair immediately seep into my energy field. It felt dense and heavy, and I began to feel sad and despondent. Focusing on the energy of my Soul, calling white light to me and filling myself up with love, I began radiating it to everyone in the room. The dense feelings of grief released from my body immediately, and the energy in the room began to liven up. People started to move around and talk to each other, when just a moment ago it was silent and gloomy. Although it was a heartbreaking occasion, radiating love to heal the hearts of everyone in the room shifted the vibration into a higher place, at least for a little while.

Love is the answer, and your Soul is filled with the most powerful, unconditional, healing love. Through love and gentleness your Soul will heal the wounds of the human experience for yourself or another. The desire of every Soul is to share its love with the world. This is true greatness!

Soul Sovereignty

A sovereign Soul recognizes the connection to God as its main source from which all needs are met. This Soul feels complete from within, and never feels lonely, even when alone for extended periods of time.

Life began to feel like a magic carpet ride as I was being carried from one place to another on a secure current of energy. It seemed the more I healed myself, the stronger a conduit I became. The energy of grace will have difficulty flowing through a dense, toxic body and will exhaust the practitioner. To be able to handle the power of God's grace will require an equal amount of self-care and inner-healing work. I was becoming an independent sovereign being. God provided everything I needed and still does.

The profundity with which life is meant to be lived may be scary or unusual at first. Yet, there is no other way to live with true love, joy, freedom, and power. For the first time in my life, I liked myself. Loving myself became a sacred relationship between God and me. The infinite source of love and creation is now my one and only true Source. God's love is incomparable as the most stable, unconditional support beyond any human being. From this sacred relationship, I became whole. My mind was liberated from ego fear, allowing inner peace to rule my world. Without judgment, I was able to release control and hold the space of love for the outer world to heal and evolve despite the chaos.

New love grew deep within my being. This love was not the same as loving a spouse, child, or animal. This love was deeply profound and connected to all living creatures, from insect to fish to human to bird to a blade of grass and the inherent right for all living things to thrive. Humans are not superior to other life-forms. My heart grew big, and love kept pouring out of it to all areas of life.

I fell in love with life. The natural world spoke to me in various ways. My lawn asked to stop using chemicals on it. The mountain ranges called to me at times and requested a visit for me to tap into their grounding energy supplies. When the ocean called, I knew it was time to tap into the vast emotional power of peace and expansion. One of my cats was getting ready to leave the Earth and gave me the time frame in which he would pass so I could prepare accordingly.

Our ancestors and indigenous people knew the meaning of nature and how to remain in balance with it. They knew every animal, insect, or tree had a purpose. They knew where to settle and where not to, based on energy vortexes in the land. They knew where to build sacred burial grounds and where to leave the Earth pristine and untouched. They knew the voices of the wind, rain, and sun, and they listened for guidance from great spirits. They knew all this, and now we must learn how to return to this sacred, natural way of living.

For me, a sanctity about life was now present. Gratitude being the foundation, self-love being essential, and world-service being inevitable. Every day a morning prayer of gratitude was spoken aloud: "Thank You, God, for all that I am, all that I have, and all that You wish to work through me." Gratitude is the foundation of life and for all things to be manifested. Be grateful for all that you have now and all that you are in this moment, as this will release feelings of lack and bring feelings of fullness. When we create our lives from fullness rather than lack, we create from a much higher vibration. Remember, you have already been programmed with greatness and your heart's desires. Everything you desire is already within you.

When this concept is embraced and integrated into your life, I promise life will automatically improve.

I wish to clarify world-service. You don't need to be a healer, author, channel, psychic medium, social worker, therapist, doctor, or anything else that is perceived to be respectable to be in service to the world. If you are a kind person who engages in self-healing to raise your vibration, you positively affect the world within the matrix of all Souls. Since we are all one Soul, one love, and created from divine love, the most potent way to affect change is to become the change you wish to see. In my view, this is the most important aspect of awakening.

With continued awakening, I cherished life, all of it. Reflecting on past hurt, I blessed each person and forgave myself. I acknowledged how the karmic nature of hurt, betrayal, rejection, and fear led to profound healing and awakening. Without these experiences, I would not be the sovereign being I am today. I was grateful for every experience that shaped me.

Souls of other people began to show themselves to my mind's eye. Beyond what people physically looked like, were their authentic selves, their Souls. The truth of who we are goes beyond color, religion, ethnicity, or education. I saw this suddenly as I sat in my car in the parking lot after making a clothing purchase. Checking to make sure the receipt total was correct after spending more than I originally intended, I suddenly looked up at the people walking by the front of my car. Lots of customers were walking in opposite directions, carrying bags of clothing. There were tall and short people, thin and chunky people, older people, babies in carriages, people wearing ripped jeans or designer pants. As I observed each person physically, something happened. The human body seemed to fade away, leaving only the Soul or aura visible to my inner eyes. A massive energetic aura surrounded each person with an array of colors; no two auras were the same. Each Soul was as unique as a beautiful snowflake. In honor of every Soul that strolled by my car, I thanked God for offering this sacred gift. Every Soul was unique, yet magnificent! So is yours.

No one is in control of your life, but you. No one is responsible for your life, but you. Anything you wish to create is within your creative power. Your Soul is a powerful, sovereign being.

Order in the Universe

As expansive as the Soul is in its connection to a vast Universe, there is much order in the energy patterns here. It is not an "anything goes" system. In fact, it's quite the opposite. I have personally found that universal order can be strict, following a fine line of ethics, love, creativity, use of power, and the understanding of what true freedom is. I've often described my path as being extraordinary and expansive, yet strict in its boundaries to comply with my Soul's unfolding. At times the ego will pop in and distort reality, creating confusion. This is unavoidable as long as we are living in human reality. In those moments, the need to slow down, pull back, and surrender is essential to getting back on track.

One of our deepest fears is to evolve and awaken due to fear of the unknown. The ego may fight hard to justify remaining in the status quo. As long as fear or false power drives any cause, it does not indicate a directive of the Soul. Divine love is so powerful it is incomprehensible to the mind. Expect resistance from your ego. Then love yourself more, and resistance will transform into acceptance. Following is a channeling through me from my master guide. The content is spoken in the voice of spirit.

A Channeling on Soul, July 2020

Greetings, dear Souls of light. I come with many other high beings of light to assist you to connect with your Soul's origin, the connection to your deepest, truest part of you that is the most important part of your beingness. We in spirit see you as whole beings, beautiful souls on a human journey, experiencing much challenge. This is destined, a Soul choice, and an agreement with Creator to bring in a new and higher levels of consciousness for your planet. Each one of you has been called to this, or you would not be here right now. You were born, we could say, from an abundant, loving, powerful Universe. In a moment when the Universe breathed, one moment of breath and consciousness was formed, a note sounded in the Universe in that moment, and from one unique sound your Soul was born. That sound and breath are uniquely yours. No other sound or breath is exactly like yours. You are a living consciousness of eternal life force that doesn't ever cease to exist. An eternal essence of pure divine love. Your Soul could be hundreds of thousands of years old. Some of you are very old Souls, and those who understand, know there is something very wise about you. Then there are the newer Souls. But the Soul in and of itself is an ageless entity created in the image of The All That Is. This is the highest version of who you are: the purity of love and light consciousness, Christ or Buddha consciousness, the Light of Divine Unconditional Love, and this is what you are electromagnetically created from. The human self is created from bones and blood and cellular matter, but the essence of your Soul is an energy that bathes itself in the essence of divine love. You are flawless energy of love, wisdom, compassion, unlimited potential, and greatness. This lives within every one of you—not some of you, every one of you. You are a magnificent co-creator with God to create the life you dream of, to create a planet with a higher level of consciousness. And in this quest to understand who you are, your Soul steps forward, and from that moment, your Soul has a purpose here. That purpose is unique to you; it is not a replication of anyone else's purpose. Imagine the formation of a snowflake. From the heavens on a snowy day, millions of snowflakes fall. You are one of those snowflakes. Unique. Different. Not one of you is the same. And yet, as millions of snowflakes fall from the same oneness, they individuate in their uniqueness only to form a blanket of white powder, symbolic of oneness and unity. This is symbolic of the light of your Soul, the uniqueness of your Soul, and yet, you are part of the whole. The beauty of fresh, newly fallen snow represents the purity of your Soul.

Innately, your Soul possesses many gifts and natural abilities, psychic, intuition, creativity, confidence, a true sense of self, who you are, and your purpose here. Your Soul is your inner healer. There is nothing your Soul cannot conquer. If there is anger and hurt within you, your Soul will replace it with love and forgiveness. If there is disease in your body, your Soul will replace it with perfect health. These are the miracles; these are the natural gifts and abilities of the divine Soul, of which you are. You are programmed for success; you are programmed to be healthy, prosperous, with love and relationships that are mutually beneficial and loving. This is your true nature. To some this may sound like a fantasy, but it is not. It is the true nature of the Soul, and it is the purpose of the human journey to remember. To walk through the valley of the shadow in human life, where the wounds of many past lives and this life originate, to heal those pieces that your Soul may form once again a beautiful blanket of white powder covering the earth in wholeness. As you open your heart to others, we say to open your heart to yourself as well. For your connection to your greatness and the being that God created you to be is the greatest gift you offer the world. It is that light and that love that hold the stability of peace and harmony and abundance. You are living in a time when this understanding is very critical; this is the most powerful human journey of all. You are light, love, joy, freedom, and power. You are everything miraculous as one of God's most blessed, sacred, and precious creations. We in spirit ask you to own and embrace this description as your true self. Your Soul has all the answers you need to live in abundance when you follow inner guidance. The higher your vibration, the easier your life will become. You'll become a magnet to attract the desires of your beautiful Soul.

Trust this process, dear ones. We are here to assist you in these evolutionary times to infuse you with love and new ideas on how to proceed. You are never alone. You are deeply loved. You are a sovereign being.

—Heshtar

Miracle 7 – April 2022

Chicken soup was on my weekend menu. I went to the grocery store to pick up a few ingredients and happened to see Dean behind the deli counter. I've known him for 6 years as he often waited on me when I needed turkey and roast beef for my kitties.

We always gave a quick wave hello when I passed by the counter. It was a Saturday evening when I saw him and walked over to ask how his job search was going. He had been a part-time employee of this grocery store for decades, but also held another full-time position as a chef elsewhere. The part-time position did offer small pension benefits which he did not want to lose. The pandemic resulted in a loss of his main source of income as a chef.

"The job search isn't going so great. I'm getting concerned. I'd love to work here full-time because I know the ropes so well, but that won't ever happen. They don't hire from within and offer management positions. You know, it's all about money," he admitted.

"I understand," I replied, feeling frustrated by this truth.

Sadly, this practice is commonplace nowadays. Hiring part-time workers instead of full time workers is due to companies not wanting to pay health or other benefits.

His eyes conveyed worry about finding a new job. He had sent out many resumes but hadn't heard from anyone. He causally expressed his concern that maybe some employers wouldn't want him. "Maybe they don't want a guy like me, you know?" he said.

I tuned into the unspoken feelings behind his words. Energetically I saw his insecurities as well as some ancestral patterns, and then felt a pang of hurt in my heart for him. "Let's keep praying," I said with encouragement.

He assured me that he always prayed to God as his momma taught him to do.

As I walked away to finish grocery shopping, God spoke to me. It's not unusual for me to hear the word of God at random moments. This time was one of them.

Clearly, in my mind I heard, "Go back to Dean."

I was shown an image of me holding his hand over the deli counter. My feeling was that God would release whatever was blocking him from attracting in a new job. He'd get a powerful healing in this moment. At first I hesitated and thought, *Hold his hand over the counter? Right now? People would think we were crazy.*

God did not speak again. Know this about God. When His word is spoken, it is up to the receiver to accept and follow or not.

I walked down the aisle and placed a few items in the cart. Then, something came over me. I swung the cart around and swiftly walked back to the counter.

"Dean, give me your hand." He looked at me strangely.

I repeated, "Give me your hand."

He cautiously reached his strong arm and large hand over the counter. I held it tightly in the palm of my small hand. He trusted me in that moment, not knowing what to expect. Instantly he closed his eyes, as did I. For less than one minute we were connected in a sacred way. In my mind's eye, I saw the Light of God's healing power run through my hand into his body ripping through insecurities and ancestral patterns. He felt the energy rush as the power of God healed him. I noticed his body slightly trembled as he let out one sigh after another. A sacred presence was orchestrating a miracle.

The deli department was without customers. God was in control of that, until a woman walked over to us and said, "What's going on here? Is there magic going on? I need some!"

I smiled, "Only a few prayers."

I released his hand from mine, and we nodded in an understanding that something miraculous had just occurred.

"I felt that!" he said in disbelief.

I nodded, "I know."

Not wanting to discuss what just happened further due to the woman standing at the deli counter, I walked away to finish shopping.

Sunday afternoon I realized I had forgotten to purchase a bunch of escarole for the chicken soup. I returned to the grocery store. As I walked into the store I had a thought, *Dean will tell me good news.* My heart felt excited that maybe he got a job. Doubting thoughts overrode the intuitive ones, *Nothing happened from last night until today – it's Sunday!!*

As I strolled down the produce aisle, I grabbed a head of escarole, then saw Dean walking briskly toward me.

"You are not going to believe this, but just this morning I received a phone call from a job I applied to over 2 months ago. They are looking for someone like me, and I can have part- time or full-time employment – whatever I want. No one calls on a Sunday morning to offer a job! It's very promising and just what I've been searching for. What did you do to me last night?"

I observed he was relieved, and was in awe of the mystery which occurred only fifteen hours ago.

"I knew it! I just knew it!" I said. "God told me to go back to you at the counter last night. I was instructed to hold your hand, and HE would create a miracle."

"I believe it! No one has ever done anything like this for me. You have a good soul," he replied grinning from ear to ear.

"When God asks me to serve, I do as he requests. Mine is not to question, but only to serve Him. You deserve to have a good job, with benefits," I said, almost teary eyed.

"May I hug you?" he asked.

"Of course! Now keep me posted! I hope you'll keep some hours here at the grocery store so I can pass by the counter to see you smiling."

I checked out at the register feeling uplifted beyond words. Walking to my car I said, "Use me, God! Use me as you wish!"

In the days afterwards, Dean received several more job offers. Then, the true miracle happened. A few days later I saw Dean behind the counter waiting on a long line of customers.

"Do you have any news for me?" I asked.

"Oh, I certainly do! And you're not gonna believe it!" He replied with excitement in his voice.

I waited about ten minutes for the long line of customers to subside, and then he walked out from behind the counter to share the good news. "Management called me into the office just this morning and offered me a full-time position as a manager! This never happens! It's so strange, but I know you had something to do with it. You're like my angel." His eyes were wide with delight.

"Oh my goodness! It was not me. It was God, and your Soul that created this miracle. It seems God had this job waiting for you all along and now you have it." I was thrilled for him.

This position included a higher wage than any other job, including health benefits, and an increase in pension benefits. He accepted the offer.

God had spoken. We were are in awe of the miracle God created within 21 days.

Since that day, I've felt elated for Dean, and in awe of how God will use us, if we allow it. Being a conduit for the divine to work through has taken many years to cultivate. I have no control over whether or not a miracle occurs. That is between a Soul and God. To be the vessel through which a miracle transpires is fulfilling beyond words.

*   *   *

Although we may always experience upheaval and discord to some degree in the world, and in our own lives, God asks us to believe in Him. No matter what is happening, miracles will be granted.

Thank you for taking the journey in the little blue healing room. May your life be transformed from the greatness already within. May you love deeply from your Soul, and never forget how special you are. Fall in love with yourself.

Conclusion: Let your faith be bigger than your fears. Never forget you are universal light. Life is challenging at times. Those moments need healing and are temporary unless we choose to wallow in the sorrow. The return to your inner light is within your power as the person you begin to love is yourself. Never let someone extinguish your light. You were not created to be dimmed. The light of your Soul illuminates the world with love.

EPILOGUE

Evolution is occurring. Through every personal, community, or global crisis, we take a small step forward toward the understanding that we are unified through our Soul's connection with the Universe. When we heal from crisis, forgive through compassion, we awaken the deepest aspect of our Soul nature—love.

Through every crisis, thousands of people wake up to realize the only way forward is to heal the wounds of the past so as not to repeat history. Our lives are but moments in time, reflective of the karmic journey our Souls have chosen to heal through human life. It's challenging, yet rewarding and necessary if we wish to create a more abundant future.

What would it be like to live without worry or fear, disease, poverty, or war? To live with abundance, prosperity, and good health? Every desire we have is rooted in one true desire; to remember the loving nature of our Soul, for all forms of life. In truth, the Soul was created to live in its greatness in co-creation with God. We have come to understand just how possible this is, not as a dream, but as a reality come true. To love ourselves fully we must stay the path, even during the most challenging times, and transform our ego wounds into the wholeness of being—love, joy, freedom, and power.

We desire world peace, human and animal rights, a clean

Earth offering organic foods rich in nutrients, a healthy body able to live with longevity, and eradication of disease. To accomplish these desires we must continue to evolve beyond the current third dimension (limitation, lack, disease, war, separation) and fourth dimension (intuition, psychic, connection to spirits). We must reach the fifth-dimensional reality, where disease, poverty, hate, war, and the ignorance of separation do not exist. Love, peace, health, prosperity, and abundance represent our Souls' true nature in the fifth dimension. This is where true spirituality will be understood. There is much inner work to be done to integrate fully the higher nature of who we are as powerful Souls.

Perhaps we must ask Creator what we need to create in our world rather than creating what we think we want. Our world is filled with creations of the ego rather than the Soul. The natural world of nature and beauty has been encroached upon by overdevelopment. We are out of balance with nature in many ways. We are stewards of the Earth; we do not own the Earth. As the Soul awakens, we will use our co-creative powers to create something very different from what we see today. This is where evolution is taking us. With an open mind, and complete surrender to a higher power, evolution will pave the way.

Higher dimensions of reality are more available to us now than ever before, thanks to many pioneers who are working hard to heal themselves and create a new Earth. Divine love, miracles of healing, unity, prosperity, and peace are within our reach, yet they will not happen overnight. We the people will create the future from who we are now, and who we are evolving into. The future depends on how we love and heal in this moment. If there is no personal evolution, the future will not become as we dream it to be.

It may take hundreds to thousands of years before this vision is fully manifested. Currently we are releasing the Piscean Age, an age of ego desire, religious conformity, and co-dependence on others including government. We must not be discouraged. We should forge ahead with each other and with God as our guide. To fulfill the destiny of the Age of Aquarius, which will be more firmly integrated by 2030, we must be willing to expand out of old-paradigm beliefs about who we are and why we are here. Before the new age of freedom, love, unity and equality can be anchored in, we must walk through the valley of the shadow of Aquarius, which is where we are now. We cannot ignore the shadow; it is through darkness that the light of awakening occurs. Evolution of the new age brings forth the ability to release ourselves from past karma, free ourselves from human suffering, and create the great awakening of the Soul. Raising our vibration for the collective awakening is critical now and for the future. Our world will not change until we change ourselves.

We have experienced another global crisis, COVID-19, beginning in 2019—another karmic experience to trigger deeper fears for human evolution to occur. Fear is our biggest enemy as it causes us to react in defense of the ego. Fear reduces our bodies' immune system and clouds our abilities to think clearly and be rational, making us vulnerable to the opinions and control of others. Fear puts us in survival mode, closing off our connection to Heaven and Earth, creating anxiety, which can result in making decisions that we later regret. Most of all, fear shuts off our abilities to connect with our true power and inner Soul guidance. When our internal ego-fears, including death, are recognized as illusions, we will shift our Earthly realities into peace. Then we will no longer need to experience such tragic circumstances. It is possible to evolve through peace rather than fear. This is our choice.

Through the COVID-19 experience, the collective was reminded of what really matters. First and foremost, that we are all connected through compassion. The entire world was and still is in chaos, reminding us we are all in this together. Gratitude is the foundation for the simplest things, and everything we currently have. The importance of building a strong immune system and taking care of the body was and still is key to good health. We were reminded that nothing in life should be taken for granted. Nothing is owed to us. Life is fragile and nonpermanent. The only way to live is in connection to God.

We are currently living in a world divided by institutions and media. We are experiencing karmic upheaval which can't afford to be divided by hatred, or our differences. Any institution, person, or group creating the division is our problem. Hatred will never bring unity or peace, it will only create more hatred and division. We must rise above the discord and return to unity.

I believe that our codependence on people and institutions—especially government—to take care of us prohibits our true power from awakening. If we turn our power over to something other than our Soul, and God, we are disempowering ourselves. We must never allow others to control us or take our power away. At this time in history we are experiencing a Great Awakening of humanity, the awakening to the truth about who we are, and why we are here. The Great Awakening will illuminate how we've been conditioned to give our power away, and those who want usurp that power. We will take our power back. We are evolving beyond the old-paradigm patterns of fear and codependency, and awakening to our true power as Soul beings. Be loyal to your Soul, and God, not the outer world of illusion. Be unified in your heart; we are all ONE. We were born to live in freedom.

In 1994, my mom was diagnosed with multiple myeloma, a rare bone cancer. Back then, life expectancy was five years at most. Mom was the only family member who believed in my work and wanted to live to see my book published. I asked God to keep Mom alive for as long as it took to finish the book. Again, I bargained with God, and he delivered. At the time, I had no idea the manuscript would take eighteen years to complete. God's timing is always the right timing. Mom continued to astound doctors with her ability to overcome active cancer cells. She had been through more chemo treatments and surgeries than I can count. Yet, she pushed on with enthusiasm for life.

In the last few years, I became my mom's healer. I listened to her life stories as she ruminated over the good times, and the not so good times. Memories of disharmony were surfacing to be healed before her destined departure. We spoke daily at great lengths, as I held space for the pain of her life to be released. There was no reason for her to carry that baggage forward. One day while sitting at her kitchen table she said, "Pauline, you have healed me. You have listened to my stories of pain and hurt, and somehow, I feel free of them." I gently held her hand in mine, and a sigh of relief swept over me. My prayers for her had been answered.

In March 2021, mom made a difficult decision to stop all medications, including chemotherapy treatment. Her decision came as no surprise, and I honored her choice to do so. She had fought long enough, and now she was allowing God to take control of her life.

"When God wants me, he will take me, and I'm ready," she often said.

We never know when the final moment will arrive, and the memories created until that time are precious. She was aware the manuscript had been completed and in the hands of the publisher. My daily calls to her always ended with, "Is the book published yet?"

I was blessed with twenty-seven years since her diagnosis. God had given us a great gift of life, hope, and a miracle. Mom passed in August, 2021, yet her spirit is alive, guiding me from above. I feel her presence every day.

I continue to follow the will of God and the destined path of my Soul. Any other life path would be fruitless. We were not created to live in limitation or lack. We were created to live in freedom, abundance, and to love each other as one Soul.

My life isn't perfect. Challenging circumstances still show up. How I respond is different and within my control. To remain centered in times of unrest requires a strong connection to divine love within our heart. Each circumstance is an opportunity to awaken more fully. Ultimately, I choose love, joy, freedom, and the power of my Soul.

Surrender your life to our Creator to be led to your greatness and true purpose. You are here to contribute to the evolution of our planet. Your Soul's light is needed.

Accomplishing this task will be humankind's salvation.

Printed in the United States
by Baker & Taylor Publisher Services